KU-784-004

# Contents

**Foreword**

# HANDICAPPING CONDITIONS IN CHILDREN

WITHDRAWN

WS 2129115 2

618.
92
HAN

JUL97

**CROOM HELM SPECIAL EDUCATION SERIES**
**Edited by Bill Gillham, Department of Psychology,**
**University of Strathclyde**

*Already Available:*

ENCOURAGING LANGUAGE DEVELOPMENT
Phyllis Hastings and Bessie Hayes

INDEPENDENCE TRAINING FOR VISUALLY HANDICAPPED
CHILDREN
Doris W. Tooze

WORK PREPARATION FOR THE HANDICAPPED
David Hutchinson

TOYS AND PLAY FOR THE HANDICAPPED CHILD
Barbara Riddick

DAILY LIVING WITH THE HANDICAPPED CHILD
Diana Millard

TEACHING POOR READERS IN THE SECONDARY SCHOOL
Christine Cassell

TEACHING READING TO MENTALLY HANDICAPPED CHILDREN
James Thatcher

HELPING THE CHILD OF EXCEPTIONAL ABILITY
Susan Leyden

# Handicapping Conditions in Children

Edited by BILL GILLHAM

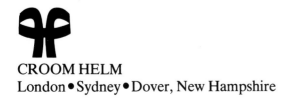

**CROOM HELM**
London • Sydney • Dover, New Hampshire

© 1986 Bill Gillham
Croom Helm Ltd, Provident House, Burrell Row,
Beckenham, Kent BR3 1AT
Croom Helm Australia Pty Ltd, Suite 4, 6th Floor,
64-76 Kippax Street, Surry Hills, NSW 2010, Australia

British Library Cataloguing in Publication Data
Handicapping conditions in children. — (Croom
    Helm special education series)
    1. Handicapped children
    I. Gillham, W.E.C.
    362.4′088054      HV888
    ISBN 0-7099-0285-9

Croom Helm, 51 Washington Street, Dover,
New Hampshire 03820, USA

Library of Congress Cataloging in Publication Data
Main entry under title:

Handicapping conditions in children.

    (Croom Helm special education series)
    Bibliography: p.
    Includes index.
    1. Handicapped children—Rehabilitation.
2. Handicapped children—Education.   3. Handicapped
children—Services for.   I. Gillham, Bill.   II. Series.
RJ138.H35    1986       362.4′088054        85-22444
ISBN 0-7099-0285-9 (pbk.)

Typeset in 11pt Times Roman by Leaper & Gard, Bristol
Printed and bound in Great Britain

# Foreword

The past decade has seen a great deal of debate over the issue of integration vs segregation of handicapped children, which in the UK has been centred on the 1978 Warnock Report. It is unfortunate that this debate has often polarised and been presented as liberal, progressive vs conservative, authoritarian. When protagonists have to defend or justify themselves the special needs of individual children can be overlooked.

One aspect of the debate, as part of the argument for 'normalisation', has been to suggest that we are all handicapped in one sense or another. Because handicap is a social or environmental concept it is easy to extend the term to include everybody; but then the term starts to lose meaning. True, one can turn the traditional view on its head by envisaging situations where we all lived in total darkness (lack of vision no handicap there) or where ceiling height was fixed at 5 feet (handicapping everyone except those under 10 years old and those in wheelchairs).

Although such conceptual games may give insight into the nature of handicap they can also play down the actual consequences of *disability*. Being black, or working class, or a woman, may be handicapping in certain social situations; but it is different in kind from being deaf or cerebrally palsied.

Much of the glibness of the debate has been due to ignorance of even the basic facts of disability. The present book sets out to present factual evidence about the nature of most of the common or well-known disabling conditions. Children who suffer from these disabilities are even more handicapped if those who come into contact with them do not understand the nature of their limitations. If there is any answer to disability it lies in an informed, adaptive response by the social and physical environment. This short book, which gives guidance on further reading in each instance, is not absolutely comprehensive, but does cover a wider range of conditions than any other available introductory text.

The Croom Helm Special Education Series is explicitly intended to let experienced practitioners communicate their knowledge and understanding to a wide audience, including other practitioners and those in training. *Handicapping Conditions in Children* is the 'key' book of the series, each chapter written by someone with a special knowledge of the subject. In the chapters on cerebral palsy and spina bifida the editor was greatly helped by the advice of Dr Margaret Drummond of the Achamore Centre, Glasgow.

## Acknowledgements

The photograph of the baby with spina bifida (p. 91) was kindly supplied by Professor Forrester Cockburn of Glasgow University; the other photographs were taken by Sam Grainger, Terry Simms and Susan Barrett. The drawing on p. 71 is by Rosanne Strachan. Dennis Vardy designed the writing slope on p. 97.

We are grateful to the following authors and publishers for permission to reproduce copyright diagrams: Churchill Livingstone for figure of EEG trace from J.M. Sutherland and M.J. Eadie (1980) *The Epilepsies: Modern Diagnosis and Treatment,* and for figure of frequency components of English speech sounds devised by Dr Mary Sheridan, from J. Ballantyne (1977) *Deafness;* Woodhead-Faulkner and the author for the diagram of the eye from A. Klemz (1977) *Blindness and Partial Sight;* Allen & Unwin for diagram of the ear from C.I. Howarth and W.E.C. Gillham (eds) (1981) *The Stucture of Psychology;* Hodder & Stoughton for diagram of a neuron and the brain from B. Gillham (ed) (1981) *Psychology for Today.*

# CHAPTER 1

# Mental Handicap

BILL GILLHAM

That an account of mental handicap is the first chapter in this book is no accident of organisation. Of all our faculties intelligence is the most fundamental: it enables us to adapt to and manage the environmental demands that are made on us, to exploit our personal resources and to overcome or bypass our limitations. Impairments of vision, of hearing, of the ability to move around, are all serious: but the handicaps posed by these disabilities can be reduced by the adaptiveness of our intelligence.

In our society we tend to think of intelligence as something to do with academic achievement, and 'intelligence' tests are commonly validated against school attainments and examination performance. But this is an excessively narrow view of human intelligence, which in fact manifests itself in a range of social-survival skills. Everyday living makes continuous demands on our intellectual judgement, and one of the weaknesses of intelligence tests is that they usually take little account of these aspects of being intelligent.

Legislation has always construed mental handicap in terms of social as well as academic competence. In the UK the Mental Health Act of 1983 represents a major advance on the earlier Acts of 1959 and 1913, but retains a broadly based definition of mental handicap — which it refers to as 'severe mental impairment' — describing it as 'a state of arrested or incomplete development of mind which includes severe impairment of intelligence and social functioning and is associated with abnormally aggressive or seriously irresponsible conduct on the part of the person concerned'.

Note that this definition is, in part, for certain purposes of the Act, i.e. to provide a statutory basis for control or institutionalisation, and so must not be taken as an adequate or reasonable general description of mentally handicapped people.

## Who Are The Mentally Handicapped?

As might be expected from the above there is no 'tight' definition of mental handicap that is generally accepted. Indeed, whether someone comes to be defined as mentally handicapped is a social process as much as anything else: other people have to have a reason or purpose for applying the label. With severe conditions there is usually consensus, but not always (e.g. 'He's not mentally handicapped, he's autistic'), but with milder conditions the label

1

becomes problematic. For example, should all children with Down's syndrome be described as 'mentally handicapped'?

Assessment on intelligence tests provides the simplest formulation, especially when the results are expressed in terms of an intelligence quotient or IQ. Linked to the IQ range are descriptive labels: the range 50-75 has usually been described as 'mild mental handicap'; 30-50 as 'severe mental handicap'; and below IQ 30 (or 'untestable') as 'profound mental handicap'. In the UK prior to the early 1970s the IQ 50 point was of great significance because children with scores below that were deemed 'ineducable' and excluded from the education system. A similar distinction obtained in the United States, where 'mental retardates' were classified as either 'educable' or 'trainable' (EMR or TMR).

IQ is a useful descriptive shorthand but it is no more than that. We cannot measure intelligence directly so the term 'intelligence' test is a misnomer. Intelligence is something we infer from performance, and we do it all the time. Intelligence tests sample attainments which are claimed to provide an adequate basis for this inference. However, no two intelligence tests are the same (although there is usually substantial overlap) so results vary. A person's IQ depends on which test he has been given.

The modern intelligence test originated in Paris in the first decade of this century. Alfred Binet and a collaborator devised an age-scale (composed of items that seemed to reflect developing intelligence at successive age-levels) and which enabled him to say, for example, whether a 10-year-old child was performing at that level or at a lower or higher level. If the child could pass test items only up to the 5-year-old level, then it might be reasonable to describe him as 'mentally retarded'.

The age-scale and the IQ score relate to one part of the basic definition of mental handicap: someone who is performing substantially below his or her age-level on intellectual attainments. In the example given above, and using a ratio formula:

$$\frac{\text{Mental Age or Developmental Age}}{\text{Chronological Age}} \times 100 = 50$$

When an intelligence test is based on an age-scale — which only makes sense in relation to children — IQ can be seen as an index of slow development. IQ, however, does not explain the condition, nor is it a measure of 'capacity', although it has traditionally been seen as such. Nor is slowness of development a sufficient definition of mental handicap. We shall return to this point later.

By school age virtually all cases of severe and profound mental handicap have been identified. The incidence is approximately 1 in 250 children. In England and Wales these children are described as Educationally Subnormal (Severe) (ESN(S)). Most children in this category are identified long before school age, and the risk or probability of mental handicap may be recognised even at birth or soon after because of evidence of brain damage.

One major difference between children with IQs below 50 and those in the range 50-75 is that the former group is much more likely to show evidence of organic impairment. The other major difference is in the social-class composition of the two groups. Children who are classified as ESN(S) are scattered across all the social classes; children who become classified as Educationally Subnormal (Moderate) (ESN(M)) are almost entirely from social classes IV and V and have been found to contain a relatively high proportion of black children. Environmental causes are, therefore, clearly important. Indeed, the validity of this category must be considered suspect since many normal schools do not seek special placement or identification for children who might otherwise be described as ESN(M). For that reason the present chapter deals only with those children whose handicap is more severe.

## Detection of Severe Mental Handicap

A number of factors determine when, and how early, mental handicap is detected:

— recognisable conditions such as Down's syndrome;
— evidence of brain damage which alerts parents and professionals alike;
— parental sensitivity: parents are often the first to detect that 'something is wrong', usually in their attempted interactions with the child;
— quality of medical and educational services, especially the quality of routine screening.

Nobody expects to have a mentally handicapped baby, and all parents know that different children vary in the age at which they reach their developmental milestones and that some are more active than others. A significant proportion of children who turn out to be severely mentally handicapped have no significant physical defects and develop normally in terms of sitting up, crawling and so on, during the first year of life. Indeed, it may only be in the parents' attempts to play with the child, and the child's lack of responsiveness, that there will be grounds for doubt about his mental development.

By the second and third year of life, when we look for language development, more definite signs of mental handicap may be apparent. But again, there is considerable 'normal' variation, and boys are noticeably slower than girls in starting to talk. Hard-and-fast deadlines are not something one can offer with great confidence. But if a child is not producing single words by 21 months and word combinations by 27 months there is good reason for seeking some professional advice, especially when evidence of language *comprehension* is uncertain. Usually, however, there will be other evidence of delay

— a failure to play, destructiveness, activity without apparent purpose, and so on.

Although, exceptionally, children who develop language around the normal time can still turn out to be mentally handicapped, delayed language is usually a key factor in the identification and definition of mental handicap. This does *not* mean that all language-delayed children should be seen as mentally handicapped. It is worth remembering that Carlyle did not speak until the age of 4 years (saying 'What ails thee, Jock?' when he saw another child crying). However, the strength of the association is shown in a study by Stevenson and Richman (1976). They took a 1 in 4 random sample of the total population of 3-year-old children living in one outer London borough. Of those identified as having language delay (language-age level below 30 months), 50 per cent also manifested retarded non-verbal mental abilities (non-verbal mental age less than two-thirds their chronological age). Thus, although it is important not to equate language retardation with mental retardation, the one warrants careful investigation of the possibility of the other.

## Causes of Severe Mental Handicap

### Down's Syndrome

About 25 per cent of mentally handicapped children have a chromosome disorder, and most of these are suffering from Down's syndrome. It must be noted here that the terms 'mongolism' and 'mongoloid' are obsolete and are considered offensive by many people, especially parents, since it suggests that the children are a race apart, an alien category.

The risk of having a baby with Down's syndrome is strongly associated with maternal age, i.e. around 1 in 1000 for women in their twenties to 1 in 100 for women in their forties. However, most Down's babies are born to young women because it is at this age that the great majority of women have their children.

The cause of Down's syndrome (a chromosomal abnormality — most usually an 'extra' chromosome 21 — hence 'trisomy 21') was first described as recently as 1959 by a group of French medical scientists. About 10 per cent of children with Down's syndrome have chromosomal abnormalities slightly different from trisomy 21, but the basic character of the condition is the same.

We are most of us familiar with the typical appearance of children with Down's syndrome, especially their facial characteristics: the slightly flattened nose and the epicanthal fold across the corner of the eyes. But there are, in fact, a large number of diagnostic features and associated conditions. The most serious of these is the common occurrence of cardiac defects — a major cause of early death. Leukaemia is also quite common, as is a heightened susceptibility to respiratory infection.

Although they almost always attract the label 'mentally handicapped' as a consequence of the diagnosis, Down's children typically score in the upper range in the IQ category of 'severe mental handicap' and commonly achieve scores in the 'mild mental handicap' to low average range. But the most notable feature of this group is that, almost irrespective of IQ, given systematic teaching by parents and professionals, their achievements in attainments such as reading are quite often within the lower part of the ordinary school range, and sometimes above that. In the UK the Down's Children's Association has promoted the enhancement of the potential of this group, who were until comparatively recently routinely considered as 'ineducable'.

There are sex-linked chromosome disorders associated with mental handicap (Klinefelter's syndrome in boys, Turner's syndrome in girls, and the well-publicised extra Y chromosome disorder first detected in adult delinquent males), but these are all rare.

### Damage to the Central Nervous System

Perhaps as many as a third of mentally handicapped children have a non-progressive brain lesion associated with cerebral palsy, spina bifida, or some other injury. Infections such as meningitis also contribute to the total. Because the extent and character of the damage is often unknown, and frequently idiosyncratic in its effects, this is a group difficult to legislate for and can present great problems in management and education. It is within this aetio-logical category that the most profoundly handicapped are usually found.

Damage is something that happens to what might have been an 'intact' child. For parents there is often the thought that 'it might not have happened' — or should not have happened. And associated with this is the desire to search for the 'cause' — what went wrong. But it is often difficult to determine causal events, so that it is a subject of unprofitable speculation. And even if the cause is identified, in terms of treatment one is none the wiser. In educational terms the necessary treatment is to take the child as one finds him and adopt a behavioural approach, modifying the programme according to the child's responsiveness to the teaching techniques employed.

*Miscellaneous Causes*

Medical textbooks list a large number of recognisable but more-or-less rare conditions in mental handicap, and these account for perhaps a quarter of the group. There is no space to describe them here, but it is worth noting that this group includes one of the rare preventive successes.

Phenylketonuria (PKU) occurs about once in 15,000 births, and is now routinely screened for at birth. It is recessively inherited (genes have to pair up) and is detected by the level of phenylpyruvic acid (or phenylalanine) in the infant's urine. Phenylalanine is present in many foodstuffs and is normally converted by an enzyme during digestion. In the infant with PKU this enzyme is missing, and unless an adapted diet is prescribed he will become mentally retarded. Untreated PKU is now almost unknown, and it is usually ultimately possible for the child to come off the adapted diet.

*Unknown Causes*

Any large group of mentally handicapped children will include 10-15 per cent for whom there is no identifiable cause, other than extremely speculative. They are identified as mentally handicapped purely on behavioural or psychological characteristics. It would not be correct to say that they look perfectly normal: if nothing else, small details like eye contact, movement patterns and social behaviour usually convey that something is wrong. But in a small proportion there are not even these indications, and the sense of mystery is very great.

**The Nature of Mental Handicap**

Is there more to mental handicap than developmental retardation in intellectual and linguistic skills? Clearly that is a primary basis for definition. But is it sufficient?

We have seen that social competence (or social *intelligence*) is long established as one important aspect of definition: sometimes being more important than intellectual retardation *per se*. Parents have always been well aware of this, professionals perhaps less so: hence the current concept of 'normalisation', i.e. seeking to avoid placements, procedures, and ways of relating to them, that make the mentally handicapped more 'abnormal' than they need be.

We have also noted the strong association between intellectual retardation and language retardation. But are these not just aspects of a general developmental delay — maturation at a much slower rate? One researcher, for example, has claimed that in Down's syndrome 'human behaviour is refracted and spread out as a spectrum'.

This 'developmental' or 'maturational' view of mental handicap is contrasted with the 'deficit' viewpoint: the idea that the mentally handicapped are deficient in their use of language, even when they have it. The primary exponent of this idea is the Russian psychologist Luria (1961), who claimed that retarded children are inferior to normal children particularly in their ability to regulate their motor actions by means of speech. He claimed that they are characterised by an 'inertness' of the verbal system (or 'second signalling system') in that it is poorly integrated with the motor system. Certainly, for all children the integration between language, thought and action appears to be important if they are to profit from the range of experiences offered by the environment. Language and action are ways in which children develop their intelligence; an 'inertness' here would compound existing mental handicap.

Empirical research indicates that a 'developmental delay' view of mental handicap is not adequate in respect of language, even when children with specific brain damage are excluded.

Gould (1976) carried out an epidemiological study of severely mentally retarded children in the former London borough of Camberwell. The children's non-verbal cognitive skills were examined on a variety of tests (because no one test was adequate for all the children), and they were assigned to an IQ range on the basis of these assessments. The data are therefore crude, but the categories are simple. Children were also divided into a 'language' or 'no language' group, being assigned to the latter if they had too little language to achieve a score on a language test and could not even compensate by using gesture. Gould's data are summarised in Tables 1.1 and 1.2.

Whilst there is a general trend (apparent in Table 1.2) for language to be positively associated with IQ level, children with 'no language' are present at all non-verbal IQ levels, and the age-trend (Table 1.1) does not show any dramatic change in the proportion of children with 'no language' in the higher age-groups.

Swann and Mittler (1976) carried out a slightly finer-grain analysis in their survey of 1,400 pupils in 19 ESN(S) schools in the north-west of England, and found that whilst younger pupils (3-6 years of age) made encouraging progress in language development, 'their subsequent slow rate of progress gave cause for extreme concern'. There was little progress in the production of single words, two-word utterances, or more complicated sentences between the ages of 6 and 16. Of the 16-year-olds studied, 22 per cent were still at the single-word stage, and 17 per cent had not even reached that level.

The fact of limited speech (or no speech) obviously presents serious problems in communication, which can only partly be met by the provision of non-speech alternatives, e.g. signing and symbol systems, described in the next chapter. Less obvious, and not so generally recognised, is the role of language in the development of intelligence: something that Piaget only gave adequate

*Table 1.1: Camberwell: Numbers of Children Attending Services for Severe Mental Retardation or with IQ 49 or Below, but Attending other Services on 31 December 1970: Language Category by Age*

| Language category | 0-4 years | 5-9 years | 10-14 years | Total |
|---|---|---|---|---|
| No language | 28 | 26 | 17 | 71 (47.3%) |
| Some language | 22 | 29 | 23 | 74 (49.3%) |
| Died before assessment | 5 | 0 | 0 | 5 (3.4%) |

*Table 1.2: Non-verbal Intelligence and Language Category*

| Non-verbal IQ | No language | Some language | Total |
|---|---|---|---|
| 0-19 | 43 | 2 | 45 |
| 20-34 | 14 | 12 | 26 |
| 35-49 | 9 | 26 | 35 |
| 50+ (non-verbal only) | 5 | 25 | 30 |
| 50+ (verbal and performance) | 0 | 9 | 9 |

Source: Both tables derived from Gould, 1976.

recognition to late in his career. Language is, of course, more than speech, and is best regarded as a system of symbols which an individual can use for purposes of thought and communication, i.e. as a means of representation. Ultimately, thought and intelligence are not linguistic but need a language system if they are to operate fully, to interact with the world of learning. The Russian psychologist Vygotsky (1962) suggests that 'thought is not merely expressed in words; it comes into existence through them'.

The significance of this interaction for the mentally handicapped is that language development is crucial if their intellectual capabilities are to be maximised. No claim for great gains is implied here. Few of us would doubt that our abilities are limited to an indeterminate extent by native endowment and, in some cases, by damage or defect as well. But how intelligent we become in practice depends upon the quality of our interaction with our environment. And it is language (both written and spoken) and related symbol systems like those in mathematics that enable us to interact, to represent, and to rework our thinking: to make use of our capabilities.

In the amelioration of mental handicap, therefore, language development (not just *speech* development) is an objective of overriding importance. The problem here is that language is not something we normally find we have to teach in any systematic or direct sense: if it were then life would be very difficult for parents. The great majority of children, however poorly served by their environment, become relatively skilful users of language at an early age; they acquire it 'incidentally'. But a general finding about mentally handicapped children, and not just in relation to language, is that they do not learn easily in this incidental fashion. This characteristic shows up in research on social-class differences on language attainments. A well-established finding is that children from the 'white-collar' classes (I, II and III non-manual) do better on all language measures than children from the 'manual' classes (III manual, IV and V). But Carr (1970) in a longitudinal study of 60 Down's syndrome children found no social-class differences in language development. And Mittler and Berry (1977), summarising the study by Swann and Mittler previously cited, in a sample of 1,400 retarded children 'failed to detect any evidence that children from "middle class" homes showed even the slightest tendency to achieve higher scores in a series of language measures than children from "working class" homes'.

## The Failure of Incidental Learning

This lack of a social-class effect on the language achievements of mentally handicapped children emphasises a qualitative difference in their learning ability, of importance for parents and educators alike. Mittler and Berry conclude their comments by saying that the lack of a social-class effect

> may be related in part to difficulties in incidental learning reported by some research workers ... It is possible that the kind of 'enriched environment' that seems to favour learning in normal children may by itself be inappropriate for severely mentally handicapped children.

The relative failure to learn incidentally and the need for structured learning experiences, including carefully structured teaching, is a widely reported characteristic of the mentally handicapped. The deficit seems to be due to a failure to attend to the relevant features of what has to be learnt or 'picked up'.

The past decade has seen a proliferation of structured teaching programmes for these children, and the 'behavioural' philosophy underlying them has been widely influential. Few schools for the mentally handicapped have not adopted this pragmatic approach to instruction. Basic to the approach is the establishment of *attainment hierarchies*, essentially an ordered curriculum specifying what the child should be able to do, e.g. in number work, in dressing himself and so on, in the order in which the skills logically develop. Thus, the curriculum is specified in terms of *behavioural objectives* for the child rather than teaching activities for the teacher (although these may be attached). Since the tasks to be learnt are often complex they have to be broken down into manageable steps for teaching and learning; this process is known as *task analysis*. Assessment is an integral part of this approach to instruction, both to assess where the child needs to start (the *entry point*), and to assess whether the child has reached a given objective.

The best known of the developmental teaching programmes based on this behavioural approach is that incorporated in the Portage home teaching programme. Originating in the United States, the programme and adapted versions of it are now widely used with young mentally handicapped children in the UK. In many parts of the country a well-organised service network has developed centred on the use of Portage. The extensive involvement of parents in this (as teachers of their own children) has led in some areas to a degree of partnership between professionals and parents which has radically changed the educational prospects of the children involved.

In the area of language and at various levels of development, a number of language programmes have emerged including the author's *First Words Language Programme* (1979) and *Two Words Together* (1983) and the *Derbyshire Language Programme* (Masidlover, 1979).

There is a limit to what can be taught specifically, in language as in anything else. There are also massive constraints on what can be taught by paid professionals on special premises. Many basic-skills programmes are constructed so as to be usable by parents as well as teachers, partly because of an awareness of the value of parents as a teaching resource for their own children and of the need to locate skills in the natural setting where they will be used, but also because a specified teaching approach increases interaction between the child and adults. One of the most difficult problems affecting the mentally handicapped child's linguistic and other development is that he effectively handicaps himself.

To an extent which is impossible to determine, language evolves out of a complex and largely unconscious pattern of communicative interaction between parent and child, so that deficiencies in the responsiveness of one partner are likely to affect the other. Research shows that mothers find it difficult and discouraging to interact with their handicapped child: and because he does not help *her*, he will get less help himself. The goals for the parents set by a teaching programme seem to support their attempts and determination to get through to their child; with incidental benefits to the child himself.

## Educational Provision

Given the learning characteristics of mentally handicapped children and their distinctive teaching needs, how are these best met? We are past the stage where we simply apply labels to children (blind, deaf, mentally handicapped, and so on) and transfer them to appropriately labelled schools. With the mentally handicapped, as with other descriptive categories, the question has to be: how are their special educational needs to be met? And we also have the less immediate question which relates to what we do in the present: how far does what we do go towards helping them to lead a more normal life?

It is not special educational placement so much as special teaching that confers educational benefits: it may be that this is most efficiently organised in a special school. Individual facilities have to be judged on their own merits. It is certainly much easier to bring together special equipment and expertise in one place, or a few places; but a school where all the children are special is an inherently abnormal environment. Adaptation there may have little relevance to adaptation in normal social settings.

Practical factors are often crucial in making a placement decision. Many mentally handicapped children are also multiply handicapped and so require care and equipment on a scale which would not be feasible in the great majority of ordinary schools. Whilst there is a trend for more mentally handicapped children to be integrated, at least at the primary level, these are usually the 'higher grade' children — most often Down's syndrome — without other conspicuous handicaps. The development of special units attached to ordinary schools and allowing a greater or lesser degree of mainstream participation, extends the range of children who can be 'integrated'. But it must not be thought that special schools are necessarily second best. Without doubt standards of teaching in ESN(S) schools have been transformed in the last 12 to 15 years, and it is no exaggeration to say that there is virtually a new profession of teaching specialists whose influence has yet to be fully appreciated.

The main gap in educational provision for the mentally handicapped is at the 16+ level. At this age most who do not obtain employment pass into the care of the Social Services Departments. There are isolated, and sometimes outstanding, educational provisions, such as the Work Preparation Unit at Worksop College of Further Education (described by David Hutchinson in his book in the present series); but in times of economic stringency we cannot look to much further development of this kind, in spite of the Warnock recommendations on grants for handicapped students (DES, 1978).

The 1981 Education Acts (separate but similar in England and Wales, and Scotland) lay down the responsibility of Education Authorities to identify special educational *needs* with the associated implication that suitable facilities and procedures be developed. The formal procedure, called 'statementing' in England and Wales and 'recording' in Scotland, includes statutory consultation with parents and the recording of their views. The full power of the new Acts is not yet apparent in practice, but the potential is there.


**Summary**

To go back to the beginning: intelligence tests, seen as measures of potential, and reflecting wider social attitudes, seemed at one time to set the limits on what mentally handicapped children could achieve. Expectation and teaching being geared accordingly, the children usually went no further than the expected level; and when they did their achievements were not taken seriously, or were regarded as curious. Except in rare cases (e.g. Butterfield, 1961), teachers and parents accepted the verdicts of medical and psychological experts.

The past 15 years has seen a revolution in the teaching of the mentally handicapped, and whilst it is important not to exaggerate what has taken place or to suggest that greater progress would be possible with all children, achievements that would once have been thought impossible are now commonplace. Much is implied in the simple fact that some children who until recently would have been classed as 'ineducable', are now attending normal schools.

It would be wrong to suggest that many mentally handicapped children can hope for population average levels of achievement. But our view of handicap has shifted. In the past mentally handicapped children have been victims of their own failure to learn incidentally (which 'proved' their defect). We are now at the stage where we can formulate mental handicap differently — without denying that the child contributes to his own limitations — in terms of the *degree of dependence on instruction*. The more intelligent children are, the more able they are to identify what they have to learn and to learn it efficiently. The intellectually advantaged child literally operates on his environment (including other people, questioning, demanding help) to make himself more intelligent: he takes the initiative. The mentally handicapped child is correspondingly more dependent on the environment taking the initiative to help him achieve his potential.

## Further Reading

Clarke, A.D.B. and Clarke, A.M. (1973) *Mental Retardation and Behavioural Research,* Edinburgh and London: Churchill Livingstone

Gibson, D. (1978) *Down's Syndrome: The Psychology of Mongolism,* New York: Cambridge University Press

Luria, A.R. (1961) *The Role of Speech in the Regulation of Normal and Abnormal Behaviour,* Oxford: Pergamon Press

Thatcher, J. (1984) *Teaching Reading to Mentally Handicapped Children,* Croom Helm Special Education Series, London: Croom Helm

Two useful organisations which can provide help and information are:

MENCAP
123 Golden Lane
London EC1Y 0RT
Tel: 01 253 9433
(provides advice and information on a wide range of matters to do with mentally handicapped people)

Down's Children's Association
4 Oxford Street
London W1N 9FL
Tel: 01 580 0511
(provides information, support and special assessment for Down's children and their parents)

# CHAPTER 2

# Disorders of Language and Communication

BILL GILLHAM

The two milestones most eagerly awaited by the parents of a young child are the first independent steps and the first independent words. Both achievements, if they occur at around the normal time, are incontrovertible evidence that several interrelated systems of the body and brain are functioning efficiently. Of the two achievements, independent language use is the more complex neurologically and is of more direct significance for normal psychological development. It marks emerging intelligence and the development of relationships with other people.

It is not surprising, therefore, that the commonest reason for a preschool child to be brought to a psychological or paediatric clinic is language delay. The great majority of such children will go on to develop language normally, without special help; they will have had a simple delay which caused temporary concern but was, self-evidently, of no particular significance. But in a minority the delay will be more enduring and may prove to be symptomatic of other conditions such as mental handicap or hearing impairment. For these reasons *all* language delay has to be taken seriously since it is only by careful investigation and the monitoring of progress that those children who need special attention can be identified.

## What is Language?

Language is most simply described as a system of symbols which we can use to represent ideas, information, wishes, intentions and the like. That much is obvious. When we use the term 'language' we are most commonly referring to speech — the *expressive* dimension. Less conspicuous, but equally important, our understanding of language (*comprehension*) is another part of the process. More covertly we also use language as an internal or *associative* process when we are thinking.

Those who have been through the school system (although not necessarily because of it) also have a second *visual* language system — written language. If the most conspicuous aspect of auditory language is speech, that of visual language is reading (the comprehension side of the process). Most people read a fair amount; relatively few do much writing of any kind (the production side of written language). This relates to fundamental differences in the *uses* of written and spoken language.

Spoken and written language are quite distinct: the latter is more formal and, by and large, they have different purposes. Spoken language is embedded in our social relationships so that it is impossible to escape from it. By the same token, not being able to speak and understand speech is a fundamental handicap, at best severely restricting social relationships, at worst creating social isolation. Competence in written language is by no means so fundamental or so obvious; which is presumably why a substantial minority of the population manage to get by without it.

Because communication is more than spoken (or written) language, it is sometimes said that we have a body language, i.e. the various ways in which we communicate non-verbally. Although most of us are very good at 'reading' the meaning of such aspects of behaviour as body posture, eye contact, gesture and the like, such indications do not constitute a language in the sense of being symbolic (which is why babies can make sense of them when they are still at the presymbolic stage of their intellectual development). Of course, gestural symbol systems (sign languages) have been developed, but these are artificial constructions and have to be learnt systematically; they will be considered later in the chapter.

## The Child With Language Delay

But what does all this imply for the child of 2 to 3 years who has been brought to our attention because he has little or no speech? Ignoring written language for the moment (although *some* preschool children with little speech show signs of recognising written words), it means that at least there is a need to assess the level of:

— speech,
— speech comprehension
— non-verbal communication,
— associative language, i.e. intellectual use of language in problem solving.

Before any of this, however, the child's hearing must be checked out very carefully. Even with the much improved paediatric surveillance now generally available, children with a significant hearing loss are still sometimes not picked up. Obviously, if sound is not getting in speech will not come out. But the situation is rarely as cut and dried as that. One of the reasons why a hearing loss is not detected is that the child hears quite a lot but has impaired hearing for speech, i.e. across the range of sound frequencies involved in speech. When what you hear sounds like a voice on the radio coming through the wall of the flat next door, you will *hear*, but not hear enough to understand and to take in to develop language for yourself (see also pp. 36-8).

Speech delay may also be the first clear indication of a mild degree of damage to the central nervous system, e.g. a mild spastic hemiplegia (see p. 65). More rarely it may indicate the condition of infantile autism, in which case it will be associated with deficiencies and disorders in all aspects of communication. Much more commonly it is an indication of general intellectual retardation.

In the majority of cases, however, the delay is specific to language; and *may* be persistent. It is almost impossible to predict with certainty in an individual case.

## The Prevalence of Language Delay

There are relatively few prevalence studies of language delay or impairment which could be considered in any sense representative of the population at large. But the wide variations in the incidence cited in individual studies are due not just to the characteristics of the sample but also to the *criterion* of delay or impairment and the *age* of the children studied.

Bearing these qualifications in mind, we can consider that the National Child Development Study (Davie, Butler and Goldstein 1972) which examined a UK national cohort of 15,496 7-year-old children, found that1.38 per cent were reported as having marked speech defects but normal hearing.

The best study of the age-level which attracts most concern (3 years or thereabouts) is that by Stevenson and Richman (1976), also referred to in Chapter 1. Taking a 1 in 4 random sample in one London borough, they reported an incidence of 2.27 per cent of children with severe expressive language delay (language age less than two-thirds chronological age), and 1.42 per cent with specific expressive language delay (language age less than two-thirds non-verbal mental age).

Whilst the comparison of the data from these two studies emphasises that language delay is largely a temporary phenomenon, it is none the less true that delayed or impaired language is one of the commonest handicapping conditions in children.

## Investigating Language Delay

If we assume that the notional 3-year-old child with delayed speech has had his hearing tested, and perhaps has had a routine neurological examination, where do we go from there? The possible character of language delay is best described by considering the processes of investigation.

*Expressive Language*

The first step in investigating language delay is to get clear evidence of how much speech a child has and assess its qualitative characteristics. This is not as easy as it sounds: speech is essentially a spontaneous form of social behaviour and so is very sensitive to interpersonal factors (strangers, uncertainty) and the situation (unfamiliar, ambiguous). Although there are some widely used language tests (notably the *Reynell Language Scales* in the UK), the validity of language data — and scores derived from them — gathered in clinic settings have therefore to be treated with caution. Parents often feel, with good reason, that the clinician has not seen their child 'as he really is'.

Apart from the uncertain validity of the language sample obtained by a standardised test, the score obtained has a spurious precision in the sense that the norms are based on *average* performance and yet *normal* development in language is wide ranging. However, since there are broad developmental norms available in the research literature, these can be used to 'place' more informal assessment data.

As a general rule it is best to use several different forms of language assessment since these usually turn out to be mutually corrective and complementary. Whilst they may not have the information available in a professionally organised form, parents are in a unique position as a source of information about a child's language; if it is their first child they will have the advantage of being able to attend to the detail of development, and with subsequent children they will have a standard by which they can compare development. This primary source of information can be tapped by carefully structured questioning, e.g.

— *Does the child imitate words (and how clearly)?*
This is important evidence of a child's physical capability for speech since it usually occurs before independent production gets under way. It is also evidence that he is focusing on spoken utterances *per se*. However, persistent imitation over a long period *without* independent speech appearing, may suggest associated mental handicap or, rarely, autism.
— *Does he have any words he says independently?*
With fewer than 50 words parents are quite often able to list them. Some parents will be helped by being given a checklist of the 100 most frequently used words by young children (see Gillham, 1979).
— *Does he put two words together?*
Parents are usually quite well able to distinguish between a genuine combination of separate elements and 'fixed' phrases that effectively operate as single words, e.g. 'wassat?'. However, they may be helped by a checklist of the most common first word combinations (see Gillham, 1983).
— *Does he put three words (or more) together?*
If this occurs at all in a young preschool child who is thought to be language delayed, it is significant since it represents considerable progress along the

*Table 2.1: Classification of Syntax Levels in Young Children*

| Stage | Approximate age | Major characteristics |
|---|---|---|
| (i) | 9-18 months | Single-word utterances |
| (ii) | 18 months-2 years | Two-word utterances |
| (iii) | 2-2$\frac{1}{2}$ years | Three main elements |
| (iv) | 2$\frac{1}{2}$-3 years | Four main elements |
| (v) | 3-3$\frac{1}{2}$ years | Emergence of complex sentences containing more than one clause, e.g. uses conjunctives. Has acquired the essential 'creativity' or generativity of language |
| (vi) | 3$\frac{1}{2}$-4$\frac{1}{2}$ years | Perfection of various linguistic systems, e.g. pronouns, auxiliary and irregular verbs |
| (vii) | 4$\frac{1}{2}$ years onwards | Still acquiring new structures up to age 7 or so. Begins to appreciate 'layers of interpretation' in language — jokes, puns, riddles, *double entendres* and so on |

road of syntactic development. In young children it is this 'upper bound' that gives evidence of a favourable prognosis for future language development.

Levels of syntax can be classified using the stages defined by Crystal (1976), a summary derivation of which is given in Table 2.1.

The results of a simple structured interview — essentially a retrospective report — can be supplemented by asking the parent to keep a written record *for one day only* on a specially prepared form (see Figure 2.1) of all the utterances a child produces. If the child is language delayed the task is not too onerous, but it is possible to use the same record with children who have more language, maintaining it for a shorter period (half a day or a couple of hours). Although this is a narrower record it is both more detailed and more precise, giving information about language use, and not relying upon memory.

Another form of assessment which permits simple comparison and more formal analysis is to take a tape-recorded language sample using table-top toys and materials, with the parents present as a support (and adviser on how typical the language sample is), but not actually taking part in the activities. Comparison of such tape-recordings can give a vivid impression of progress, but one simple form of analysis is to calculate the range of vocabulary and the length of separate utterances. The procedure for carrying out an analysis of the *mean length of utterance* is described in Gillham, 1983. Using a standard kit of toys and books, with the tester encouraging the child to respond in as expanded a language form as he is able, a minimum of 60 consecutive utterances are tape-recorded (the first 10 being disregarded as a 'warm-up' phase). The remaining 50 are analysed for the mean length of utterance (MLU) and the mean length of the 5 longest utterances is also calculated (the upper bound or M5LU). These measures are useful up to MLU of around 4; at which point, in preschool children, language delay is not a significant problem. At the earlier stages (MLU of up to about 2 to 2.5) it may be useful to take an index of

*Figure 2.1: One-day Record Forms for Child's Utterances*

INDEPENDENT WORD RECORD

| 'Public' or 'private' word | Date first used | To whom (or to what) was the word said? | What was going on? | What do you think he was trying to say? | Was it used again fairly frequently? |
|---|---|---|---|---|---|
| eyes | 5\|4\|78 | to mother | talking face to face – pointed at eyes | there are your eyes | ? yes |
| | | | | | |

SENTENCE RECORD

| Sentence | Date first used | To whom or what used? | What was going on? | What do you think he was trying to say? | Was it used again fairly frequently? |
|---|---|---|---|---|---|
| Daddy coat | 4\|10\|78 | to mother | saw father's coat hanging on peg | that's daddy's coat | yes |
| | | | | | |

vocabulary growth by calculating the ratio of *different* words in the speech sample, i.e. the so-called *type-token ratio*:

$$\frac{\text{number of different words}}{\text{total number of words}} \times 100$$

Such data are, of course, capable of a more sophisticated analysis: they can be analysed phonetically; and psycholinguists might prefer to describe utterance complexity in terms of morphemes (the smallest meaningful units of language, not exactly corresponding to 'words' or 'elements'). From a practical point of view, speech therapists might analyse the quality of speech production according to assumptions about a distinction between *delayed* and *deviant* development (using, for example, Ingram's *Edinburgh Articulation Test*). The assumption is that deviant development is a priority for treatment, although substantial evidence of the effectiveness of such treatment is lacking.

At an impressionistic level, however, successive audio recordings give comparative evidence of changes in fluency, clarity, voice quality and so on, which are demonstrably valid — and very encouraging to those concerned with the day-to-day management and care of the child.

Children with impaired speech functions are sometimes referred to as *dysphasic*, but this medical-sounding term is purely descriptive and connotes no diagnosis (other than speculative). Children who lack speech may be referred to as *aphasic* (or as suffering from *expressive aphasia* to distinguish the condition from *receptive aphasia*, this latter condition being one where the child can hear but cannot make sense of speech). Again it has to be emphasised that these terms are essentially descriptive.

An uncommon condition is that of *elective mutism* (actually *selective* mutism) where children *can* speak but do not do so in some settings, e.g. nursery or school. Whilst the child concerned may have some speech defect, the main background reason is usually some family disturbance which makes the child tense or suspicious of outsiders. The persistence of the mutism can be quite remarkable and tends to be sustained by sympathetic adults or by other children who act as interpreters or messengers. A behavioural approach — removing the attention and support, making the satisfaction of needs contingent upon the use of speech — combined with help from the parents, is usually the 'treatment' adopted.

## Language Comprehension

In the case of the child who has no speech or very little speech, the assessment of language comprehension is particularly important. No speech does not, of course, necessarily mean no *language*, but it does usually indicate relatively little language. A careful plotting of the extent and quality of language comprehension is therefore necessary, not least because it is from this base that expressive language will develop. However, the assessment of a child's understanding of the speech of others is not easy since it has to be inferred from what he does in response. And his response may be determined by factors other than linguistic ones. Formal psychological assessment, including the use of tests, is more important here than in the assessment of expressive language.

Some degree of language comprehension appears to be a prerequisite for meaningful production although understanding of the range of uses of words and sentence forms also develops *in use* — like all skills. Until comparatively recently there was a dearth of research into the relative development of comprehension and production in young children at the beginning stages of language development. It appears that the comprehension/production gap closes very rapidly between 12 months and 24 months, but is quite wide initially. Benedict (1979), in a study of eight children, found that on average comprehension development started earlier (around 9 months), and reached the 50-word stage earlier (13 months) than production (12 months and 18 months respectively). On average the children in her study were able to *under-*

*stand* 50 words before they could *produce* 10.

It can sometimes be a matter of doubt whether children understand the specifically linguistic content of other people's communications, and it is often assumed by professionals that parents are easily deceived in this respect. But Benedict found that the parents of the children she studied on the whole tended to *under*estimate their children's language comprehension.

At the earliest stage of language development, the assessment of comprehension is largely in terms of basic vocabulary comprehension. The comprehension scale of the Reynell Language Scales is of some help at this level but not sufficiently detailed or fine-grain enough at the lower end. Standardised picture vocabulary tests are also only appropriate to a more advanced level of development (although norms are provided for very young children). A useful way of assessing picture vocabulary comprehension at this early stage is to use the author's *First Words Picture Cards* (ESA-Arnold) which are based on research into the first words children use (see illustration).

If a child with little speech also has little language comprehension, the probability is that he is intellectually retarded, and further assessment using non-verbal mental tests and observational assessment of spontaneous play and other activity will be needed before that is confirmed. One possibility (and intellectual assessment will reveal this) is that the child is suffering from the rare condition of receptive aphasia (much less common than the expressive variety). Very simply, receptive aphasia is the descriptive label given to children who are

not deaf, i.e. sound is getting in, are not mentally handicapped, but cannot understand spoken language. The assessment and teaching of these children is a highly specialised business, but *visual* language approaches (including reading/writing) are often used as a way of getting language in; and sometimes, speech will emerge as a result of this.

*Assessment of Non-linguistic Abilities*

The relationship between language development and intellectual development is a close one. Both depend on the development of the processes of representational thought. For this reason some language remediation approaches attempt to foster symbolic processes on a wide front.

In the case of a child with little speech, and especially if comprehension is poor, it is a matter of some importance to see whether representational processes, particularly as evidenced in problem-solving, are also retarded. It is a difficult assessment task: the child doesn't speak so he can't give answers, or his answers may not be adequate to his intentions; and if he has little understanding of language, he cannot be judged simply on his failure to understand verbal instructions.

Psychologists have developed a number of tests which require neither expressive language when the child makes his response, nor the understanding of language when he is presented with the task to solve. Most of these tests have been designed for use with deaf children of school-age or near it (e.g. the *Hiskey-Nebraska Test*); there is little specifically for young children. Probably the best test to use with very young children is also a very old one — the *Merrill-Palmer Scale of Mental Tests* — which is largely non-verbal, or minimally so, and is made up of items that can be given more or less independently, e.g. completing jigsaw puzzles and peg boards with differently shaped pegs. Despite its limitations it is normally sufficient to show whether or not a child is likely to be mentally handicapped.

Piagetian stage-theory provides a framework for inferring intellectual level from the spontaneous or elicited activities of young children. In the normal age-range from 12 months to 36 months, one would expect to see manifestations of representational thought in children's play and other activities, for example:

— searching for something that is absent or being surprised when something is missing;
— engaging in pretend (symbolic) play, like pretending that a box is a car or giving dolls imaginary food;
— engaging in deferred imitation, i.e. copying someone when they are out of sight;
— making rudimentary drawings or simple models out of clay or plasticine.

Parents often have an instinctive sense of when their child has done something 'intelligent' and their account of such incidents is part of the evidence.

*Assessment of Communication Abilities*

Most children with delayed or abnormal language development are fairly efficient at communicating with people who know them well: to the extent that it is sometimes suspected (almost certainly incorrectly) that they don't need to talk. The desire to communicate, and the ability to devise means of doing so, are fundamental to language development. Thus, the investigation of the extent and character of non-verbal communication skills is extremely important.

The assessment of these abilities depends partly on interview with the parents or caretakers: in particular to clarify how the child makes his wants or intentions known, but also to get a general picture of the child's social interactions with others. The development of communication is rooted in the desire to relate to other people: language builds on this. Language has three strands in its development: the specifically 'linguistic' bit, the ability to acquire and produce the units of language, words and sentences; intellectual development, the ability to represent mentally and to organise knowledge; and the ability to communicate with others that develops fom the earliest social interactions. The presence or absence of any of these functions, to a greater or lesser degree, has implications both for diagnosis and remediation.

The child with little or no language and communication abilities and who shows little interest in interacting with people is either profoundly mentally handicapped or autistic. In both cases the prognosis is not good. Indeed, the prognosis in autism is directly related to the amount of language present, even though language use may be abnormal (see Chapter 8).

## The Causes of Language and Communication Disorders

If priority has been given to the investigation of language delays and abnormalities rather than to the consideration of causes, it is because, at the level of practical action, one is little the wiser for identifying causes even on those rare occasions when one is able to do so. Language is probably our most complex psychological and neuromotor set of functions, but inferences about cause, other than hearing loss, are almost entirely speculative, and lead to no treatment consequent on the 'diagnosis'.

It is true that areas of the brain have been identified as relatively specific to speech production (Broca's area) and comprehension (Wernicke's area); but it is rarely possible to identify a localised lesion — and there is no medical treatment available if one has. Although speech therapy is commonly seen as a paramedical profession, its methods are essentially educational/psychological, and have become increasingly so.

With conditions such as cleft palate, corrective surgery can improve the ability to speak, but popular assumptions that children with poor articulation are suffering from 'tongue-tie' are erroneous, the problem being more profound than that.

Language delay and impairments commonly run in families, but the mode of inheritance is unknown and the contribution of environmental factors difficult to determine. Whilst the effects of the social environment on language are manifest they are rarely fundamental. The drive towards language is so strong that even children in highly abnormal linguistic environments, e.g. with two deaf parents, will usually develop normal language. This is not to deny environmental effects, but to show that they are unlikely to account for the fundamental levels of language handicap being considered in this chapter.

## Approaches to Language Remediation

Psychologists, speech therapists and the like are very much better at assessing a child's linguistic and other abilities than they are at doing anything about them. But it is likely that direct remediation does not lie in their hands. It is most improbable that brief, if regular, sessions with a 'specialist' (e.g. half an hour weekly with a speech therapist) can have any effect at all on a preschool child's language.

The evaluation of all forms of preschool intervention is patchy, but the broad trend of the evidence is that effects are gained (and maintained) to the extent that parents are involved and are the main agents of change. School, because it is a major and daily feature of children's lives, can also be influential where its activities are focused and regularly maintained as a form of special support: in practice not easy to achieve.

The situation is not as grim as might be inferred from the foregoing because the great majority of children with delayed speech learn to speak satisfactorily. This is not the case with children who have associated mental handicap, so that this group is a priority for language help. Very difficult to identify with any predictive confidence are those children, not mentally handicapped, who will have continuing language problems. For this reason, continuous monitoring is necessary.

Approaches to language remediation are numerous, but broadly vary according to the extent that they are *programmatic*, i.e. involve specific teaching/training sessions, objectives and methods, or *naturalistic*, i.e. seek to enhance natural language-learning opportunities. In practice a combination of both approaches usually applies.

In the programmatic approaches there is disagreement about the extent to which (and the way in which) children are required to produce speech as part of the method. Behavioural training methods place emphasis on word production and reinforcement for doing so. At one level these methods are successful — more words are produced in training sessions. But the vocabulary acquired in this way often fails to generalise to real-life settings, which is the necessary criterion for the success of such an approach. Even if the vocabulary taught is 'environmentally useful' and understanding of use is also taught, the child is still learning two things about language which are inappropriate: that language is something produced by adult demand, and that speech should be followed by reinforcement.

'Getting the child to say the word' has great commonsense appeal, and can lead to parents and others encouraging a child to engage in a great deal of naming behaviour, e.g. pictures in books, which is only a small part of normal language use, and is usually produced *spontaneously*, at the child's volition.

Because of this awareness that language remediation attempts should respect the child's control of his own language, a number of approaches emphasise the importance of language *modelling* — words and sentence forms that the child can observe and use as he sees fit — and the development of *comprehension*, so that the child learns the range of possible uses of the items modelled.

A premature emphasis on production fails to recognise that it can have an inhibiting effect on a child who is learning about language but is having difficulty in achieving speech, and that speech is the culmination of a wide range of achievements, not the beginning but the end of a relatively advanced stage of language development. It is easy to make criticisms like this, but inappropriate language interactions arise out of a basically abnormal situation. A great deal of research shows that the parents of language-delayed children speak to their children less, and less easily, than to linguistically normal children of the same age. In other words, the children concerned are compounding their own handicap. It is of little use to advise parents to make a global special effort (to 'flood their child with language' or some such) because this cannot be sustained and is of doubtful value anyway.

For language and communication to flourish it has to have a purpose. Between parents and their children this means that special or additional reasons for interaction have to be found. The simplest approach to this, since language-delayed children are often delayed in other respects, is to help parents to work with their children on several fronts where the need to speak and communicate successfully will necessarily arise, i.e. there will be a necessary increase in the level of meaningful interaction.

That is an indirect approach. More direct approaches are also required. But special efforts can only be maintained (and are probably only useful) for short periods of time. Parents can be asked to set aside, say, two 20-minute periods a day when they can concentrate on communicating with their child. At the preverbal stage this will mean such things as turn-taking play activities — a basic kind of communication — and engaging in imitation games (the adult imitating what the child does or 'says' spontaneously, and the child being encouraged to imitate back).

As evidence of language comprehension begins to emerge, the parent can focus on particular words or topics which are likely to form the child's later *spoken* vocabulary (as described in the author's *First Words Language Programme*). A great deal can be done at this stage of prespeech in working

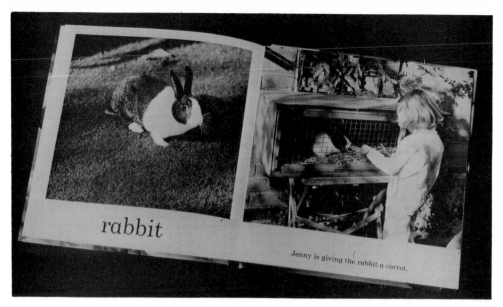

rabbit

Jenny is giving the rabbit a carrot.

on language. An insufficiently recognised language source at this level is the intellectual and linguistic input available from books. This is well described in a particular case by Dorothy Butler in *Cushla and Her Books* (1979) (see also Dorothy Butler's *Babies Need Books* (1980)). The author's *First Words Picture Book* and *Early Words Picture Book* (see illustration) cover the words research has shown most children use first when they start to speak — and which they are preparing for at the prespeech, comprehension stage.

Parents are often puzzled why a child who *can* speak (i.e. has imitated), and clearly understands some words, doesn't use them to speak for himself. The answer is that there is a big difference between comprehension adequate for recognition and comprehension adequate for recall (as in speech): the latter is much more difficult. Consider your attempts to use a foreign language; when someone speaks to you, your task is simply to understand what has been said. But if you want to speak you have to recall and reconstruct the language needed. Hence the need, in language-retarded children, for comprehension training past the level of simple comprehension to the level where the words go in and stay there, ready for use.

In normal development, vocabulary growth is slow up to the first 50 words and then accelerates from that point. Although the time-scale is different, the same usually applies to language-delayed children. But normally the 50-word stage also marks the beginning of genuine word combination. Some language-delayed children, however, at the same stage of development, do not see the potentiality of *combining* words so easily. These linked words may range from the obvious and familiar like 'drink gone' to instances where the meaning is known only to the child and perhaps his mother, e.g. 'jam home' — which translated means 'I want the jam doughnut now I'm home'. With children who have a range of single words but are slow to begin putting words together it may be necessary to adopt programmatic approaches (e.g. the author's *Two Words Together*, Masidlover's *Derbyshire Language Programme* (1979), Crystal's *LARSP* (1980)), which attempt to model sentence usage at various levels of complexity for the child to adopt.

*Non-speech Alternatives*

Whether children improve by themselves or are helped in that process by the efforts of parents and professionals, the fact remains that most of them progress. But there are a small number of children who make painfully slow progress, or none at all — usually the mentally handicapped or cerebrally palsied. For this group, if only for purposes of basic communication, some form of non-speech alternative has to be considered. This is one area where there has been widespread development in the past decade (see, for example, Jones and Cregan, 1986). Essentially there are two forms, visual symbols (however displayed) and manual signs.

In the UK and the USA there are well-established sign languages for the deaf, although for historical reasons American Sign Language (ASL) is quite different from British Sign Language (BSL) (see also pp. 44-6). The use of BSL in the UK with children who are not deaf but have limited speech is a comparatively recent development, having been promoted under the label of MAKATON, which is essentially a vocabulary subdivided into 'developmental' stages geared to using BSL. This has been extremely successful with mentally handicapped children and is now widely employed in special schools.

A much more sophisticated and elaborate signing system is that devised by the late Sir Richard Paget and subsequently adapted and further developed by Pierre Gorman. In reply to the criticism often levelled at traditional sign languages that they do not mark all the features of normal English grammar, Paget-Gorman has a consistent grammatical system (marking tense, plurals, possessives, etc.); it also has a logical system for deriving words in that, for example, all the animal words have a similar related-sign configuration. However, Paget-Gorman is restricted in its usefulness by the demands it places on the child who has to learn it; and on those who have to understand it or learn how to teach it.

All signing systems depend on a degree of voluntary control of hand movements and so are not appropriate to many cerebrally palsied children without speech. The other defect of signing systems is that they are not readily acceptable or understandable to other people, except in the special environments of schools or other institutions. It is particularly difficult to get them adopted in any general way in families. In part this is linked to the common fear of parents that by teaching a non-speaking child signs you will deprive him of the *need* to speak. The evidence is strongly in the other direction: if anything, the increased ability to communicate through signs motivates the child to explore other ways of communicating — including speech.

Visual display symbols in a variety of formats are an alternative means of

*Figure 2.2: Blissymbols*

communication for those children who can do no more than point or operate a simple electronic control. Written words, either on their own or attached to pictographs (pictorial symbols), are commonly employed. A distinctive pictographic system which has achieved wide acceptance is that known as Blissymbols (see Figure 2.2). Though originally designed as a peace-promoting international language of understanding by the Australian pacifist and idealist Charles Bliss, it has been readily adapted to the needs of the handicapped and is now the most widely used symbol system in the UK.

There are other symbol systems and all have the capability of being linked to conventional written words so that, if the symbols themselves are not immediately obvious to 'outsiders', it is of no consequence.

Symbol systems are more 'open' than signing systems, but if they are dependent on cumbersome display boards they are restricted in the sense of not being readily portable. At the present time, however, due to the rapid advances in microtechnology, we have the exciting prospect of developing open-communication alternatives to speech that are easy to carry around. Hand-held vocabulary and sentence stores with output via visual displays or voice synthesisers are already available and will increase in sophistication and ease of use. For those children capable of using them the potential is very great.

But what technology cannot do is make up for a lack of communicative intent in a child, the inability to make voluntary movement, or the failure to develop representational thought of a kind that can be shared with others.

## Further Reading

Cooper, J., Moodley, M. and Reynell, J. (1978) *Helping Language Development*, London: Edward Arnold

Crystal, D. (1980) *Introduction to Language Pathology*, London: Edward Arnold

Hastings, P. and Hayes, B. (1981) *Encouraging Language Development*, Croom Helm Special Education Series, London: Croom Helm

Reynell, J. (1980) *Language Development and Assessment*, Lancaster: MTP

The Association for All Speech Impaired Children (AFASIC)
347 Central Markets
Smithfield
London EC1 9NH
Tel: 01 236 6487
promotes the interests of all children with specific speech and language disorders.

# CHAPTER 3

# Hearing Impairment

JULIET BISHOP AND SUSAN GREGORY

Hearing loss is a major handicap, not chiefly because of its direct effect of cutting the individual off from the world of sound around him, but for the indirect effect of the problems encountered by the deaf child in learning language and the consequences of this upon other areas of development.

However, in any discussion of the needs of deaf children, the heterogeneity of the group presents problems in that any simple description of the consequences of the disability is not possible. Hearing impairment can be total (although this is actually very rare), ranging through all degrees of hearing loss to that so mild that it does not even require an aid. One in a thousand children has a severe hearing loss, and just under two in every thousand have a sufficient loss to warrant the use of a hearing aid. Intermittent losses due to ear infections and the build-up of fluid in the middle ear are also a major source of problems in the school-age group. If these various types of losses are considered along with the range of different home backgrounds, intellectual ability and personality, the extent of the difficulty of presenting a simple view of hearing impairment in children can be appreciated.

## The Physiology of the Ear

In order to understand the different types of hearing loss and their consequences, it is useful first of all to consider the structure of the human ear. A simplified diagram of the ear is shown in Figure 3.1.

It is usual to consider the ear as divided into three parts: the outer, middle and inner ears. The outer ear is made up of the pinna (the part of the ear that can be seen on the side of the head) and the ear canal, which is between 1-1$\frac{1}{4}$ inches (25-31 mm) long and ends at the eardrum (tympanic membrane). The eardrum separates the outer and middle ear, which is an air-filled cavity containing three small bones or ossicles called the malleus, incus and the stapes. The middle ear is ventilated by the Eustachian tube, a narrow passage which connects the nasopharynx (the space at the back of the nose) to the middle ear. When the two Eustachian tubes that connect each ear are functioning normally the two middle ears are sufficiently ventilated and the air pressure is equal on both sides of the eardrum. The bony fluid-filled cavity (snail shell-like in appearance) adjacent to the middle ear is known as the inner ear. This

29

*Figure 3.1: Simplified Diagram of the Ear*

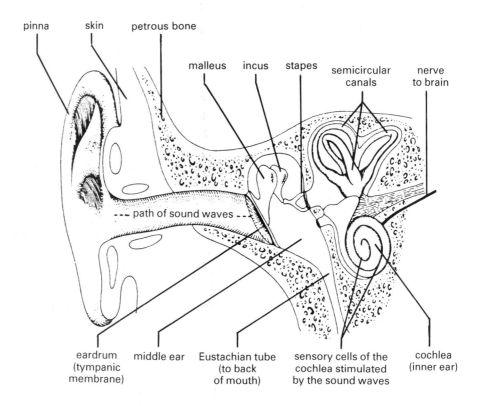

houses the delicate nerve endings that are stimulated as sound waves are transmitted through the fluid in the inner ear. These messages, translated into nerve impulses, travel along the auditory nerve to the brain for analysis and interpretation.

## Types of Hearing Loss

Sound is conducted through the air into the outer ear reaching the eardrum, which vibrates in response to sound; these vibrations are transmitted via the ossicles to the inner-ear fluids. For obvious reasons, this part of the hearing mechanism, up to the oval window (beyond the stapes), is known as the conductive pathway, and hearing losses caused by damage to, or blockage in this pathway are called *conductive* losses. However, if the sensori-neural pathway, which starts at the oval window and comprises the cochlea, auditory nerve and associated brain cells, is damaged, the deafness is known as a *sensori-neural* hearing loss. Some hearing impairments are a combination of sensori-neural and conductive losses and are known as 'mixed hearing losses'.

## Causes of Deafness

### *Sensori-neural Deafness (Perceptive Deafness)*

Sensori-neural deafness can be present from birth (congenital) or acquired during the course of development. In cases of both congenital or acquired sensori-neural hearing losses, where there is permanent damage to the cochlea, auditory nerve or auditory tracks in the brain, there is little hope of alleviating the condition medically or surgically. Such losses can be hereditary, caused by a genetic abnormality, leading to deafness as a single handicap or part of a syndrome. It is estimated that the cause of deafness is genetic in about half the cases of children born deaf. The advice of a genetic counsellor is often sought when such deafness is diagnosed since future children may be similarly affected. Congenital sensori-neural deafness can also result if the mother contracts German measles or another viral infection like influenza, during the first three months of pregnancy. Prematurity or a difficult and arduous birth resulting in an oxygen deficiency, or acute jaundice in which the mother's blood group is incompatible with that of the foetus, places the child at risk of developing a hearing loss. Acquired sensori-neural hearing losses can result from viral infections in childhood — measles, mumps, influenza, and most commonly meningitis, although the incidence is low and has decreased dramatically over the past 20 years.

### *Conductive Deafness*

Most commonly, conductive losses are acquired during infancy, early childhood or adult life, and can be caused by a build-up of wax, a foreign body, or swelling in the outer ear. The majority of conductive-hearing problems, however, are located in the middle ear. Conductive deafness caused by an acute inflammation of the middle ear, *acute otitis media*, if treated promptly with antibiotics or other medication is usually successfully alleviated, but when the inflammation persists and grows worse a condition known as *chronic otitis media* develops. This can lead to the eardrum and ossicles becoming inefficient or even damaged. Surgery involving removal and reconstruction of the middle-ear tissue and bones may be necessary to stop the inflammation from continuing. *Secretory otitis media* is very commonly the cause of intermittent partial hearing losses in children under 12 years old. Often, the problem starts with enlarged adenoids, infection in the back of the nose and throat or an allergic reaction causing a blockage at the top of the Eustachian tube which prevents air passing into and ventilating the middle ear. The air pressure in the middle ear becomes negative in relation to the pressure of the air outside the eardrum and fluid collects in the middle ear. Inhalants or nose drops are usually successful in treating the disorder. If left untreated, however, the fluid becomes thick and glue-like, and may need to be surgically alleviated by the removal of the adenoids and drainage of the fluid from the middle ear. The surgeon makes a small incision in the eardrum, drains the fluid by suction, and then fits a tiny middle-ear ventilation tube called a grommet. By the time the eardrum has healed and pushed the grommet out, it is hoped the fluid will have dispersed. For many children, however, the condition does recur, especially if an allergy is the underlying cause.

Another cause of conductive deafness is *otosclerosis*, caused when the stapes grows and becomes fixed in the oval window so that sound waves cannot be transmitted to the cochlea. Again, surgical intervention is usually successful.

Congenital conductive deafness is rare, but can be sustained in the womb during the critical time when the ear is developing, and very occasionally the cause is genetic. Children may be born without or with only a partly formed outer ear, eardrum or ossicles. For many children the damage is in one ear only, and so with help they can learn to compensate for this.

Conductive losses tend to be of a lesser degree than sensori-neural losses and as such, may not be picked up. Children may be variously described by parents or teachers as ignorant, naughty, bad tempered, disruptive, or language delayed, before their hearing loss is detected. Since at least 20 per cent of all children suffer from a conductive hearing loss in their early years, the problem is not an insignificant one. Language acquisition and progress in school can be affected if treatment for it is delayed or repeatedly unsuccessful.

Once informed of the problem, parents and teachers can act in practical ways to help the affected child; for example, making sure that he does not sit at the back of the classroom, and checking that he has understood instructions and explanations. Extra sensitivity in reading and language work is particularly useful. In extreme cases where the loss persists, hearing aids may be fitted until the condition subsides.

Since conductive losses are usually of an intermittent nature they are often first noticed by parents rather than during routine screening procedures. The main emphasis of screening, however, is to detect sensori-neural losses, and once diagnosed and their degree established, they can be ameliorated in part by the use of hearing aids.

## Screening and Diagnosis

In this country and others there is often an unnecessary delay in the confirmation of congenital deafness and subsequent fitting of hearing aids. In a survey by the Commission of European Communities it was suggested that parental suspicion of the handicap, although an important pointer to earlier diagnosis, was often ignored. In the year of the above survey (1977), although 29 per cent of infants in the UK were suspected of deafness under one year of age by parents, only 11 per cent were confirmed as actually hearing impaired by professionals. On average, only 50 per cent have their loss confirmed by their third birthday and, for some, usually those with a lower degree of loss, confirmation is not made until they enter school. These, and other findings, suggest a need to improve the implementation of screening and other diagnostic procedures used by professionals working with the hearing impaired.

For the most part, children will first be screened for hearing loss at 6-9 months of age in local health clinics, generally by health visitors, using a test known as the 'distraction test'. This involves the infant turning towards, and hence indicating he can hear, standardised sounds of high, medium and low frequency. The accuracy of the distraction test has been much questioned, but in trained hands it still remains one of the best available methods of screening large numbers of children. If the results of the test suggest that a child has a hearing problem in either or both ears, a follow-up test to confirm or disconfirm the suspected loss should take place as soon as possible. If the child still fails to respond he should be promptly referred for more sophisticated testing by specialist audiometricians who, as well as using distraction tests, will usually take a detailed case history. If it appears that the apparent deafness is one symptom of general developmental delay, he will be referred to a Paediatric Assessment Centre for a thorough examination.

When a child has reached the age of 18 months it is possible to extend the testing repertoire by incorporating a test of his active responses to quietly spoken instructions. In this 'co-operative test' the tester, positioned 3 feet (1 m away from the child's ear, may give instructions to place toy objects in various named locations, e.g. 'put the brick in the box'. This test also examines the child's language comprehension skills, which are likely to be disrupted by a hearing impairment. By the age of 30-36 months distraction tests and simple co-operative tests are usually abandoned completely in favour of more sophisticated 'performance tests'. In the performance test the child is taught to perform a particular activity (e.g. to put small wooden men into a longboat) when he hears a certain sound spoken to him over headphones. By 3 years old 'Pure Tone Audiometric Tests' can be used in which pure tones are presented with and without headphones to the child using an audiometer. A range of tone frequencies representative of those experienced within speech are presented (250, 500, 1,000, 2,000, 4,000, and 8,000 Hz), and children are required to indicate whether they can hear them. In this way the test gives the audiometrician a reasonably reliable guide to hearing ability in the important speech-frequency range. Screening for hearing loss is usually carried out during the early school years using performance tests of this type. As with distraction tests, if co-operative or performance tests suggest a hearing loss the child is usually referred on for more detailed investigation.

Once children recognise and know the names of familiar toys and pictures, their ability to hear and comprehend speech can be tested. If a child shows consistent difficulties in discriminating particular speech sounds the tester is alerted to the possibility of a particular type of hearing loss. Then as children grow older, more sophisticated speech tests can be used.

*Recent Innovations in Diagnostic Procedures*

A recent innovation is the experimental introduction of neonatal screening devices such as the 'Auditory Response Cradle', in which babies' involuntary responses to sound are measured in the first few days after birth. The results of such tests give paediatricians an indication of whether further testing of hearing is advisable to confirm a suspected loss. Researchers are optimistic about the effectiveness of such techniques, but until evaluation is complete, screening at birth will be available for only a minority of babies born in Britain.

Another neonatal screening device is 'Brain Stem Electric Response Audiometry' which involves measuring, using carefully placed electrodes (on the scalp, forehead and mastoid bone) the tiny electric signals generated by the auditory nerve in response to sound stimulation. This is a technique especially useful for testing unco-operative babies or mentally handicapped children on whom performance tests are difficult to carry out.

*Electrocochleography* is another sophisticated diagnostic technique in which the child is anaesthetised while a tiny electrode is passed through the tympanic membrane (eardrum). The tip of the electrode is placed on the bony covering of the cochlea, and when a sound stimulus is applied the action potential in the auditory nerve is recorded from the electrode at different sound intensities. This test can be used reliably with sound frequencies above 2,000 Hz.

## The Audiogram

An audiogram is a type of graph onto which a child's hearing profile is mapped. It is valuable to understand something of the nature of acoustics before an explanation of the layout of an audiogram is given. One important quality of sound is its *frequency*. When a guitar string is struck it will vibrate and move to and fro a certain number of times per second. Frequency, measured in units of Hertz (Hz), is a measure of the number of cycles of vibration exhibited by a source of sound each second. If a sound source vibrates at 500 cycles per second, its frequency would be 500 Hz. The lowest tone audible to the human ear has a frequency of 20 Hz. As frequency increases we notice a rise in pitch. Middle C on a piano has a frequency of 256 Hz. As frequency rises beyond 20,000 Hz the sound becomes inaudible or is heard merely as a hiss. Low- and high-frequency sounds have low and high pitch respectively. Although pure tones (sounds with one single frequency) are used for testing hearing, the sounds in our everyday life — music, birdsong, human speech — are complex sounds made up of combinations of pure tones.

As our sensation of pitch is affected by the frequency of a tone so our sensation of loudness depends on what is called the *intensity* of a tone. Intensity is measured in decibel units (dB). A tone which can just be heard is a 'threshold sound' and has a power of 0 dB; a whisper is around 30 dB; normal speech 60 dB; and a pneumatic drill 100 dB. When sounds reach a power of 120 dB (e.g. the noise of a jet engine) or louder, discomfort will be experienced by the listener. So the properties of sound frequency and intensity influence the way a listener hears a particular noise.

Audiometers (instruments used to test hearing and produce audiograms) are standardised using a large sample of healthy, normally hearing people, and their average threshold values for test frequencies are adopted as the normal thresholds for hearing. Each audiometer complies with the same standards. So in a 'Pure Tone Audiometric Test' of hearing (see above) the child's hearing sensitivity is compared with the average or 'normal' values obtained during this standardisation.

An audiometrician tests a child's hearing by noting on an audiogram form the point or threshold at which he hears a tone of a given frequency and intensity measured in Hz and dB respectively.

*Figure 3.2: A Sample Audiogram*

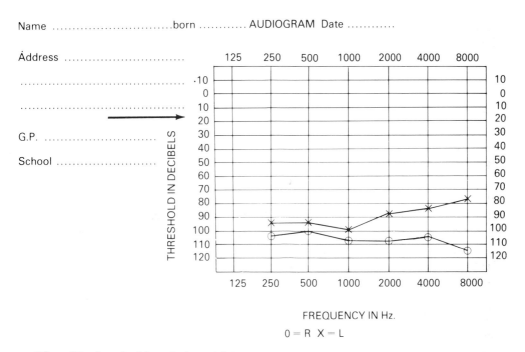

The dB thresholds of the child's hearing at six frequencies important to speech are recorded on the audiogram as shown above. An 0 is used to denote the right ear responses and an X the left. Usually (although practices do vary) the average hearing loss for a child is calculated by averaging the loss in dB over the six tested frequencies (if responses are obtainable) for each ear. The lower of the two scores (the average loss in the better ear) is taken as the child's hearing loss.

Four sample audiograms (for the left ear only) have been plotted on one audiogram form (Figure 3.3) to show something of the variety of possible hearing profiles. All have different implications for the quality of sound the child perceives. Although it is difficult to make generalisations, as an approximate guide we could say that when an audiogram indicates a loss of around 30-35 dB it is likely the child will have some difficulty hearing quietly spoken speech; hearing aids are not usually fitted in such cases since they would probably distort or make sounds too loud for the child's comfort. With losses in the 35-45 dB range, children are beginning to have difficulty hearing normal speech; whereas at 60 dB, although the child would be aware of speech sounds, without the use of amplification or lipreading, it is unlikely that he would be able to interpret them. By 80 dB even loud speech becomes indecipherable without amplification, and by 120 dB it is suggested that the child hears only grossly distorted speech patterns.

*Figure 3.3: Four Sample Left Ear Audiograms*

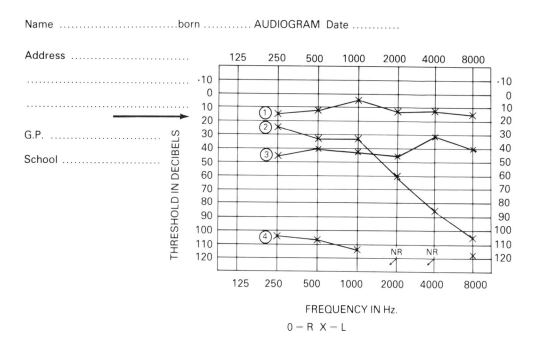

*Guide to audiograms*
1.  Normal hearing
2.  This is often described as a 'ski-slope loss' because of its general shape. The individual has some hearing for the low and moderate frequencies but poor hearing for high-frequency sounds.
3.  This is a flat and moderate loss.
4.  This audiogram indicates an individual with only 'islands' of hearing and no response (NR.) at some frequencies.

*Classification of Hearing Loss*

There are several ways in use of classifying hearing loss, but the one recently endorsed by the British Association of Teachers of the Deaf (BATOD, 1981) takes into account not only average loss in the better ear but also age of onset of hearing impairment. Prelingual loss is defined as a loss originating before the age of 18 months.

*Slightly hearing impaired*: children whose average hearing loss, regardless of age at onset, does not exceed 40 dB.
*Moderately hearing impaired:* children whose average hearing loss, regardless of age at onset, is from 41 to 70 dB.
*Severely hearing impaired*: children whose average hearing loss is from 71 to 95 dB, and those with a greater loss who acquired their impairment after the age of 18 months.
*Profoundly hearing impaired*: children who were born with, or who acquired before the age of 18 months, an average loss of 96 dB or greater.

In Figure 3.4 the speech sounds of English have been superimposed upon a standard audiogram to give a very rough idea of how certain losses affect hearing for speech.
Although speech sounds are made up of combinations of tones within the speech frequencies, vowel sounds are usually lower in frequency and higher in

*Figure 3.4: The Frequency Components of English Speech Sounds*

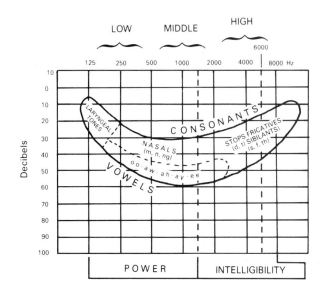

Source: Diagram first devised by Dr Mary Sheridan and taken from *Deafness* by John Ballantyne, Churchill Livingstone, 1977.

intensity than consonants. The consonant sound 'th' (as in 'thing') is the faintest sound in speech; whereas the vowel sound 'aw' (as in 'jaw') is the loudest, being nearly 30 dB on average. Vowels are the powerful sounds in speech since whilst consonants are mid- to high-frequency sounds, vowels mostly lie in the low- to mid-frequency range. The intonational contours of a sentence are conveyed largely by the vowels, and this is important in that it puts across the general meaning or tone of the sentence (whether it is a statement, command, etc.). Consonants, more than vowels, serve to distinguish one word from another.

Whilst an audiogram can give important pointers to which sounds of speech a child may have difficulties hearing, and an idea as to the type of hearing aid most suitable, it should be borne in mind that it is only one small clue to determining the deaf child's ability to discriminate speech sound. Inner-ear damage has a differing distorting effect from child to child, and many factors like past experience, use of hearing, age of diagnosis and so on, will influence speech perception. This explains, in part, why even when two hearing-impaired children are matched in a number of ways (age of diagnosis, intelligence, home background, etc. as well as hearing profile) one may have poor, and the other highly intelligible speech.

## The Hearing Aid

Hearing aids cannot correct a child's hearing loss in the way that spectacles can correct most visual impairments, since they can do no more than amplify the sounds he is physically capable of hearing. The hearing aid is only a miniature microphone, amplifier and loudspeaker designed to amplify sounds that are present in speech.

### Conventional Hearing Aids

Aids can be worn on the body, clipped to clothing or in a harness (body-worn aids) or behind the ear (post-aural aids). The conventional hearing aid has a microphone which picks up sound waves and converts the signals back to sound waves. These amplified sound waves are then delivered through the ear mould to the eardrum. The whole system is powered by batteries and is susceptible to the usual faults that beset any delicate electronic mechanism in extensive daily use.

Together with an on/off switch, aids have a volume control, enabling the user to adjust the sound reaching the ear to a comfortable level. The frequent existence on some aids of a low-, middle- and high-frequency tone-adjustment control (located inside or outside the aid) means that hearing aids can be adjusted to accommodate different hearing profiles.

The ear mould is a very important piece of the hearing aid since it must fit the ear perfectly, otherwise the sound leaks out around it, becomes re-ampli-

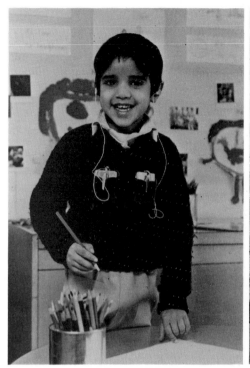 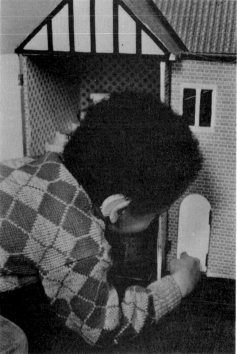

fied, and causes a shrill, whistling sound. Moulds need to be replaced regularly as the ear grows.

The conventional hearing aid has an optimum operating distance of about one yard (1 m) or less, and it is important to remember that it amplifies all sounds within its range: the loudest being those close to the child. So if, for instance, a child is sitting next to a humming fish-tank and at some distance from the teacher, the sound of the fish-tank will be amplified most, perhaps even obscuring the teacher's voice.

### Radio-microphone Hearing Aids

In recent years hearing aids employing a radio microphone have become more readily available. They are designed to overcome the problem of amplification of all sounds in the vicinity since they have the facility to selectively amplify the voice of the speaker when required.

Radio-microphone hearing aids like the 'Phonic Ear' shown in the photograph (p. 40) are made up of a radio receiver which picks up and amplifies radio waves which are generated by a microphone/transmitter worn by the teacher. They can also act as a conventional hearing aid, enabling the child to hear his own voice and those of others around him. When working as a radio microphone and conventional system, the child can hear these latter sounds but also no matter where the teacher is, up to a distance of 100 or more yards (100 m), her voice is as clear as if she were next to him. This can have interesting repercussions if the teacher forgets to switch the aid off when she is talking to other individual children in the class, or to fellow teachers in the staffroom! The microphone should be worn 6 inches (15 cm) from the mouth and switched on and off as required, since the child is in radio contact with the microphone wearer as long as the transmitter is switched on.

### Group Hearing Aids

Some schools for the deaf and partially hearing units (see later) make use of 'group hearing aids' when classes of children are taught together. Group aids, which are headphones connected by leads to a control machine, like radio aids, are designed to ameliorate the problem of background noise and teacher-child distance, but unlike with the latter, the group aid limits the user's mobility to the length of the leads on the head set.

*The Loop System*

A loop system is a mechanism which helps to get a better performance from the hearing aid in certain situations. It is used in theatres, assembly halls, living rooms, etc. and consists of a length of wire arranged around the perimeter of a room and connected to the loudspeaker output on a radio, television or tape recorder. The electrical impulses in the wire are picked up by a special coil located in the hearing aid, and the child thus hears a superior quality of sound anywhere in the 'looped room' without interference from background noises.

## The Young Deaf Child

In order to understand the later educational problems of the young deaf child, some of the difficulties that are experienced in the preschool period are worthy of consideration.

In an interview study (Gregory, 1976) of 122 families with a young deaf child, 76 per cent of the mothers expressed their major problem as being one of communication. If one looks at the figure for the amount the children could say and understand this becomes clearer. In line with the more usual practice in this country, none of the parents were being taught or encouraged to use a sign language with their children. Of the $3^1/2$ to 5-year-old group in the study, only just over one-fifth were putting words together into sentences while two-thirds had fewer than 5 words, some of these none at all. It is easier in an interview situation to find out who, rather than what, deaf children can understand, and in this same $3^1/2$ to 5-year-old group less than a third were able to understand almost anyone, while nearly a quarter could only understand their mothers. Some of the children could understand no-one at all.

The consequences for family life of this poor communication are many and various and only a few will be mentioned here. One area, and one with problems most commonly associated with it, is general socialisation and discipline. Although 'yes' and 'no' can be communicated to most deaf children, the 'whys' and 'wherefores' of life are more difficult to get across. What is acceptable behaviour, of course, often depends on context; so whilst picking wayside flowers is usually acceptable, picking one's neighbour's daffodils is unacceptable. The difference is subtle, difficult to explain, but can be crucial. Without the 'ifs', 'buts' and 'becauses' which usually temper the socialisation experiences of the hearing child, the deaf child may find the world a very arbitrary place, which cannot but be reflected in some way in the quality of his thinking.

Not surprisingly then, deaf children in their early years are more likely to experience frustration due to not understanding or not being understood, which often finds expression in temper tantrums. At $3^1/2$-5 years they are twice as likely to have regular tantrums than their hearing contemporaries, and these tantrums persist for some well beyond the age of 5 years.

Another area which can be affected by impaired hearing in the preschool years is temporal organisation, both in the prelinguistic period where sound provides the structure for many anticipation games, and later when language is used to talk about past, present and future. A normal part of most children's lives is talking about past and future events: telling Daddy the happenings of the day, anticipating a trip to the seaside, and so on; and this can be difficult for deaf children. Many mothers report their inability verbally to prepare their children for both pleasant and unpleasant experiences because of their children's poor comprehension skills. Difficulties in talking and thinking about things which are not in the here and now can persist and have consequences for later development.

**Educational Provision**

Most families with preschool hearing-impaired children will be visited by a peripatetic teacher. This will usually consist of weekly visits of about an hour in duration during school term time, although provision varies among local authorities. Peripatetic teachers offer help and guidance on language and communication development, with some teachers interpreting their role more widely and talking with families about all aspects of the deaf child's development. Teachers may work with children themselves or discuss with parents various activities they could pursue in the home.

Some authorities offer other services in the preschool period such as parent courses, mother-toddler groups or playgroups. Some hearing-impaired children may be placed in a nursery school attached to a school for the deaf. Such placements are usually full-time, full-day placements involving daily travel in a provided minibus or taxi. It is rare now to place preschool hearing impaired children in residential nursery schools for the deaf. Even with the obvious benefits which preschool experience confers, starting school can be a particularly traumatic experience for the hearing-impaired child. If he enters a special school or partially hearing unit at some distance from his home, he will not only have the usual stress of separating from his mother, an experience which may, as mentioned earlier, be impossible to explain in advance, but also of experiencing a car journey with comparative strangers. Many hearing-impaired children enter school not only emotionally and behaviourally immature, but also with very restricted communication skills. This means that unless special efforts are made by parents and professionals involved to link his experiences at home and school, the child can lead two separate lives in the two settings.

*School Placement*

The hearing-impaired child, regardless of degree of handicap, can find himself in any of a number of different types of placement. In the first place, there are residential and non-residential schools for the deaf and partially hearing throughout the UK covering the primary and secondary age range, with around 3,800 children in these schools. Although some offer a 'grammar school' type provision for the more academically able, many special schools, especially those offering residential places, have become centres for the additionally or multiply handicapped child.

Although not all local education authorities have special schools for the deaf, most have partially hearing units attached to normal schools, which, despite their name, take children with all degrees of hearing loss. Around 4,200 children attend partially hearing units throughout Britain. There has been a notable trend over the last decade for fewer children to be placed in schools for the deaf and more in partially hearing units, and this has led to the closure of a number of the former. In fact the pattern of placement emerging now, in line with recent educational legislation, is to place hearing-impaired children, wherever possible, in normal schools. In most counties this means that the more severely hearing-impaired children are placed in partially hearing units attached to normal schools, and the less impaired children in local schools, with varying degrees of resource support.

Not all partially hearing units operate on the same principle; some work on a classroom model, where all the hearing-impaired children in the school are based in the unit, going out into mainstream classes for 'integration' commensurate with their age and abilities. Other units work as resource bases within the school, withdrawing hearing-impaired children from the mainstream classes in which they are placed, for extra language work.

*Integration*

As noted above, many hearing impaired children are being placed in local primary schools. In 1975 there were 10,500 children, sufficiently deaf to wear hearing aids, integrated into classes in ordinary schools in the UK. However, the most recent figures from a survey by the British Association of Teachers of the Deaf (BATOD, 1984) indicate that in January 1983 there were 19,992 hearing-impaired children placed in normal schools and being visited by peripatetic teachers. In a few local authorities profoundly and severely hearing-impaired children as well as those with less severe handicaps are being integrated. There is considerable variation in the extent to which support is given to schools accepting a hearing-impaired child: some schools receiving weekly visits from a teacher of the deaf, others receiving additional help from part-time or full-time, school-based specialist or ancillary staff. Placement in normal schools is something which cannot be undertaken without considerable forethought and planning. Staff in the school may need access to information and support services before the child enters school and during his stay. Teacher training centres and in-service training centres will need to be geared in the future towards providing information for teachers who will increasingly expect to teach children with special needs.

## Language and Communication

The educational attainment of the deaf in this country, as well as in others, is low, although with regard to basic intelligence (as measured by non-verbal intelligence tests) there is no reason to think that the deaf are less able than the rest of the community. In a national survey of deaf school leavers (Conrad, 1979) nearly half the children studied had speech which was 'very hard to understand' or 'effectively unintelligible'. The study also showed that the median reading age of deaf children leaving schools in England and Wales is around 7-8 years. These figures form part of a profile indicating poor comprehension and use of written and spoken language on the part of the deaf child, together with underachievement in mathematical skills.

For the past two or three decades deaf children in this country, regardless of school placement or degree of hearing loss, have been educated chiefly by oral means. As the name implies, the oral method employs speech and lipreading by and with the deaf child. Considerable emphasis is placed on early and consistent use of high quality amplification and auditory training (training in speaking and listening skills) to encourage the child to use any existing residual hearing. One of the stated aims of this method is to enable deaf children to cope in the hearing world.

The whole question of mode of communication and subsequent language acquisition is seen by many parents and teachers of deaf children to be the central concern of the preschool and school years. The issue of whether deaf children should be educated totally by oral/aural means or whether this should be supplemented by sign language (a manual approach) is open to debate. If a child has a reasonable degree of hearing and does not have any additional debilitating handicaps, it is generally agreed that an auditory-based language system (an oral approach) will be adopted at home and school. If, however, a child has considerable hearing loss it is sometimes felt appropriate to use a manual means of communication to accompany speech, particularly when the low language attainments of deaf children are taken into account.

There is considerable and long-standing controversy concerning the value of the two different approaches, oral and manual. Parents usually adopt the orientation of the services from whom they receive guidance and counselling in the preschool years, and the services in turn are influenced by future educational considerations, notably the means of communication used in local authority schools in which children will be placed. Before considering this issue in more detail it is necessary to outline the manual methods that are available.

### *Manual Methods of Communication*

Manual communication systems are receiving renewed attention not only from linguists and other related professionals, but most significantly from the deaf community itself. Within most countries or communities deaf people have their own different sign languages (British Sign Language or BSL in the UK;

American Sign Language or AMESLAN in the USA; and so on). These are languages in their own right, not necessarily having the same structure as the national language of the country. The use of these languages may be supplemented by the use of fingerspelling, particularly for proper names or more unusual words. Fingerspelling uses a different hand configuration for each letter, and is used to represent the words of spoken language. Not all fingerspelling systems are the same: some use one hand and some two; for example in the UK fingerspelling uses both hands whereas in the US it uses one.

AMESLAN is used by three-quarters of deaf adults in the USA, but in a survey in the UK only 15.4 per cent of children were depending, according to school staff, on manual means to communicate. It must be recognised, however, that many deaf people begin to use signs to communicate in adulthood. Although the status of sign languages as true languages has been open to doubt in the past, this is changing, and they are used by a significant proportion of deaf people to communicate with one another. There appears to be a growing trend in some areas of the country to introduce a manual communication in the preschool years.

As well as the sign languages evolved by the deaf community, other systems for manually coding English have been derived or contrived. Some of these are based on BSL and involve taking the individual signs from BSL and combining them following English word order, and supplementing this with fingerspelling to give a manual representation of English. The most common of these is Signed English, though there is also Signs Supporting English (SSE), Seeing Essential English (SEE) and others. A very simplified system of signs adapted from BSL called MAKATON is sometimes used by and with the mentally handicapped.

Paget-Gorman signing system is another artificially contrived system (see p. 26). The uses of this language with the deaf have not been widespread, although it does serve a definite function with the language disordered.

Cued Speech differs from the manual systems already detailed in that it is intended to supplement spoken language rather than replace it. One of the problems confronting a deaf person wishing to lipread is that many sounds which appear similar on the lips are in fact different (e.g. 'm', 'b', 'p'). Cued speech attempts to use various hand configurations near to the lips to disambiguate the lip movements, and theoretically gives the listener a complete and visually intelligible message. A similar system is the Danish Hand-mouth System. Both Paget-Gorman and Cued Speech have strong proponents and can give examples of success using their system, but neither have become established in any major way.

### Oral vs Manual Methods of Communication in Education

In a recent policy statement of the British Association of Teachers of the Deaf it was agreed that one of the primary aims of the education of hearing-impaired children should be the mastery of spoken and written English. They saw this ideal of 'oralism' as achieving two broad approaches: *natural* and *structured* oralism. The former involves deaf children acquiring language in a purely natural way 'following the same process as hearing children'. The primary feature of this approach is that in natural oralism deaf children develop speech not through direct teaching but through natural auditory experience. Structured oralism is a method of teaching speech through systematic structured intervention in the child's language-learning process. Proponents of oralism stress the need for the child to be integrated into a hearing society and the fact that most deaf children have hearing parents. They also point out the difficulties that can arise in learning to read if signing is the major means of communication.

Those who favour manual means of communication for severely and profoundly deaf children stress the consistently low achievement of these children in the traditional oral approach. They differ, however, in which manual means they would apply. The majority favour a 'total communication approach' using signs to supplement speech. There is a smaller group who advocate education through BSL as being the natural language of the deaf, with spoken English being learned as a second language. The debate has continued for many years and is unlikely to reach a simple resolution. It is probably the case that no one approach is appropriate for all deaf children. Whether we shall ever evolve a flexible enough system to take into account the needs of all deaf children and families remains to be seen.

## Computers in Special Education

The microcomputer is as much a part of the special as it is the normal classroom. Together with the usual educational software packages there are a variety of available special speech training techniques like the Visispeech machine shown below.

With the use of a microcomputer, television and additional specialised hardware, the deaf child is provided with a visual display of his speech patterns and therefore a visual feedback to compensate, at least partially, for the auditory feedback he lacks when speaking.

CEEFAX is another combination of television and computers, enabling viewers with special receivers to switch to a number of pages of printed information to accompany normal television programmes. Some television subtitling is also obtainable through CEEFAX, providing the older deaf child and adult with a valuable information service.

Facilities are improving for hearing-impaired school leavers with better support being made available in certain further education colleges. In January 1983 around 842 hearing-impaired individuals occupied full-time placements in such establishments, but much still needs to be done to improve existing resources in post-compulsory education for the handicapped.

Fortunately, there is a growing awareness of the handicap conferred by deafness, partly because of increasing publicity about handicaps in general, but especially because hearing-impaired children are sharing classrooms with hearing peers. Perhaps this, more than any other process, will bring about the changes in attitude towards deaf people which are necessary for their greater participation in society.

## Further Reading

Freeman, R.D., Carbin, C.F. and Boese, R.J. (1981) *Can't Your Child Hear?*, Baltimore: University Park Press/London: Croom Helm (Raises and discusses may problems faced by parents of deaf children, and favours a total communication approach.)

Nolan, M. and Tucker, I.G. (1981) *The Hearing Impaired Child and the Family*, Human Horizons Series, London: Souvenir Press (A good book for basic information about hearing loss.)

Quigley, S.P. and Kretschmer, R. E. (1981) *The Education of Deaf Children: Issues, Theory and Practice*, Baltimore: University Park Press (An account of the various issues that are discussed when deciding on good practice with deaf children.)

RNID (1976) *Methods of Communication*, London: RNID (Currently being used in the education of deaf children.)

Somerset Education Authority (1981) *Ways and Means 3* (co-ordinated by Ann Jackson), published on behalf of Somerset Education Authority (A resource book of information, technical aids, teaching materials, and methods used in the education of hearing-impaired children.)

Further advice and information can also be sought from:
The National Deaf Children's Society
31 Gloucester Place
London W1
Tel: 01 486 3251

# CHAPTER 4

# Visual Handicap

ALLAN DODDS

## Definition

The term 'handicap' has been defined as 'a disadvantage for a given individual, resulting from an impairment or a disability, that limits or prevents the fulfilment of a role that is normal for that individual'. In terms of visual handicap this means that the visually impaired person is likely to suffer certain disadvantages in the sighted world. These may take a number of forms. For example, the individual may be unable to orient himself with respect to the environment; to move about effectively in his surroundings; to engage in a number of occupations; to integrate successfully in the social world; or to be economically self-sufficient.

A visual handicap can arise from a considerable number of causes, ranging from eye conditions which are comparatively mild and commonplace like squint (strabismus), to the fortunately rarer ones such as total blindness. Visual handicap embraces the terms 'partial sight' and 'blindness' and, as a label, it emphasises that vision is likely to be impaired rather than totally absent. The term 'blindness' is itself very misleading. In fact it has been estimated that only about 10 per cent of the blind are unable to see anything at all. The reason for this apparent contradiction between the label and its real-world referent is that 'blindness' and 'partial sight' are legal, rather than medical terms, and they are based upon the limited although none the less important criteria of whether the individual is able to carry out an occupation for which sight is essential (in the case of the adult), or whether he is likely to benefit from sighted methods of education (in the case of the child).

### Registration

The registration of a visual handicap, although not compulsory, is desirable as it enables the family of a visually handicapped child to gain access to the many services available, whether they be statutory or voluntary. In the UK registers are kept by Social Services Departments, and it is through those departments that specialist counselling and provision may be obtained, either directly or indirectly. If a child is suspected of suffering from a visual disorder, then anyone may approach the local Social Services Department requesting that an investigation be undertaken to see if the child qualifies for registration as blind or partially sighted. Once this initial step has been taken, an appointment will be made for the child to be examined by a consultant ophthalmologist, who must complete the Form BD8, which is forwarded to the local Director of Social Services. The local authority will then arrange for a qualified social worker to visit the parents to explain the various services available, including financial benefits where appropriate.

Whether the child is registered as blind or partially sighted depends upon the result of the ophthalmological investigation. It has already been stated that 'blindness' and 'partial sight' are legal rather than medical terms, but in practice, whether one is assigned to one category rather than the other depends primarily upon the degree to which the eye condition impairs the ability of the eye to resolve fine detail. If, on examination, the child is found to have an acuity of between 3/60 and 6/60 of normal vision *after correction*, then provided that there is no additional defect he will be registered as partially sighted. If his acuity is found to be less than 3/60, he will be registered as blind.

The numerical expression of acuity looks complicated but is really quite simple to understand. The term in the numerator refers to the distance (in metres) at which the child can read the appropriate letter on an eye chart: the term in the denominator refers to the distance at which a normally sighted child would be able to read the same letter. So that the child who is found to have 2/6 vision needs to be as close as 2 metres from a letter which the normally sighted child can see from as far away as 6 metres. However, consideration is also given to the integrity of the visual field (i.e. the *area* of vision). If there is a substantial field loss, then one may qualify for registration as a blind person even though one's acuity is better than 6/60. An example of this would be a person with tunnel vision and near-perfect central acuity.

## Incidence and Prevalence of Blindness

The condition of blindness has been recorded as far back as the time of Homer, and there are many references to blindness in the Bible. This is not surprising since endemic diseases which result in total blindness have existed in the Middle East and Asia for probably as long as civilisation itself. It has been estimated that there are between 10 million and 15 million blind people in the world today, and the greatest prevalence is in the Third World where parasitic infections and malnutrition compound one another. By the year 2000 it is anticipated that this number will have increased to over 30 million. Even this staggering figure represents a conservative estimate of the magnitude of the problem, since it includes only those who are totally blind. If those who have a severe visual handicap are included (and this would be of such a degree as to make them eligible for registration as a blind person in the UK), then there are probably nearer 40 million blind people in the world today.

Britain's contribution to this figure, in comparison, looks almost insignificant. In 1976 there were approximately 100,000 registered blind and 42,000 registered partially sighted in England and Wales. Of those, over 70 per cent were over the age of 65 years, and over 50 per cent were over the age of 75 years. The incidence of blindness in this country also reflects the skewed age distribution. In the infant of under one year of age the annual registration rate was just around 4 per 100,000 of the population, compared with an overall rate of around 26 per 100,000 in 1968. If one looks at the very elderly, this figure rises to around 700 per 100,000 of the population. Visual handicap may therefore be seen globally as a problem for the Third World, and domestically as one associated with the ageing process.

Given, however, that registration is not mandatory, these figures must be treated with some caution. Cullinan (1977) has estimated that 34 per cent of those eligible are not on the blind register, while 20 per cent of the partially sighted also fail to register. One notable trend observed during the period 1969-76 was an increase in the number of partially sighted registrations of young children in the 0-4-year age-group, at a time when the number of births was actually declining. There are two possible reasons for this. In the first place, advances in perinatal medical care can result in the survival of an infant with multiple handicaps, one of which may be visual. Secondly, there may be a move to earlier registration, and this question will be considered later.

**Causes of Blindness in Children**

Blindness can affect anyone, irrespective of age or social class. Many instances of blindness in adults and children alike can be attributed to simple trauma, which at the time may appear relatively trivial. Sympathetic ophthalmia is a condition in which an injury to one eye can lead to blindness in both. The only way to prevent this happening is to remove the injured eye, a decision requiring much experience.

Apart from trauma, the causes of blindness in children tend to differ from those in adults, and more frequently result in total blindness. The most common cause of blindness in young children is some failure or other in the normal development of the eye or some part of it. This is due either to an inherited defect or to the effects of viruses or toxins on the developing foetus. Since the eye develops over a period of 6 months, it is at risk during its various stages of development.

If the precursor of the eye, the optic vesicle, fails to develop within the first few weeks of life, then the whole eye may be absent at birth (anophthalmos). Alternatively, and more commonly, the eyes may be much smaller than normal (microphthalmos), and though vision may not be too severely impaired initially, as the structures within the eye grow, later blindness can be an inevitable consequence.

Another developmental defect is one involving the pupil of the eye. Commonly, a notch (coloboma) appears to have been cut out of the iris. If the defect is confined to the iris alone then vision need not be badly affected, but if it extends to other structures, a severe visual impairment can result. Sometimes the iris may be entirely absent (aniridia), and this can cause glare and discomfort in bright light (photophobia).

Glaucoma is a condition which can affect children, in which case it is usually present at birth, unlike the adult form which appears later in life. Congenital glaucoma is caused by a fault in the internal drainage mechanism of the eye, resulting in a build-up of intra-ocular pressure. Since the infant's eye is highly elastic, the eyeball takes on a bulging appearance (buphthalmos), and the infant suffers much pain. The condition can often be rectified surgically, but unfortunately with nothing like the success rate observed in the adult form.

Congenital cataract is a condition in which the development of the lens is interfered with by some external agent, for example the rubella (German measles) virus. The cataract is particularly likely to develop between the 6th and 12th weeks, and other parts of the body may well be affected. The virus can also cause deafness and mental handicap. Fortunately, inoculation can now prevent a woman from contracting the disease, but the practice is by no means universal. Termination of pregnancy is the only alternative if contact with rubella is suspected during the first 12 weeks after conception.

Retinoblastoma is a malignant condition which has a strong genetic component. It usually appears at around 2 years of age, although it can be present at birth. It may be noticed first of all by the parent as a small, white reflection in the pupil, or as a slight squint. If early treatment is not investigated, the tumour cells will travel along the optic nerve to the brain, resulting in certain death. On the other hand, early removal of the eyes can save the infant's life.

Before moving on from the more common causes of early blindness, the case of RLF is worthy of mention. During the 1950s a disproportionately large number of blind children began to appear on the register, all of whom had been born prematurely, and who were found to be suffering from a condition known as retro-lental fibroplasia (RLF). Subsequent research established that the condition, in which blood vessels in the retina grow out into the vitreous humour and subsequently atrophy, was produced by administering high levels of oxygen during the first few weeks of life. Thus, an advance in perinatal care which allowed very premature infants to survive was purchased at some considerable price. Although the cause of RLF is firmly established, it still occurs, although in much reduced numbers.

Any child whose parents suffer from any eye disorder, or whose grandparents were similarly affected, stands a greater chance of having an eye disorder himself. Sometimes the visual defect does not manifest itself for some years, and it is only when the child has grown into a young adult that the first hint of a problem can arise. In the case of the condition known as retinitis pigmentosa, which is a genetically transmitted defect of the visual pigment, the hitherto normally sighted individual begins to notice that his night vision is not as good as it used to be. This is because the rods in the peripheral visual field

*Figure 4.1: Diagram of the Human Eye*

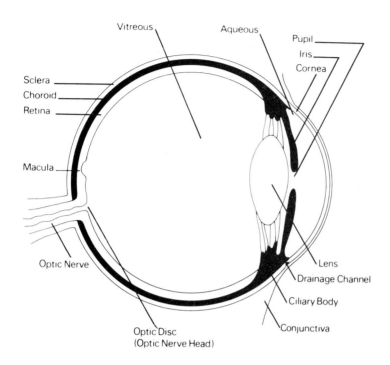

Source: Reproduced from A. Klemz (1977) *Blindness and Partial Sight*, Allen & Unwin.

are the first to be affected. The next noticeable problem is that the visual field becomes progressively restricted, until only a small tunnel of usable vision is left. Total blindness may then follow, although this is not always the case. This is a particularly distressing situation, and one which can only be avoided if the parents realise that they themselves are sufferers, a fact which may emerge too late for them to do anything about it. Anyone suspecting that his or her family has a history of eye problems of any sort should be encouraged to consult a genetic counsellor before going ahead with having a family, although many subsequently choose to ignore the advice given, especially in the case of those who have themselves grown up from birth as blind people and who will never understand why the sighted regard blindness as such a handicap.

**Blindness in Infancy**

Being visually handicapped certainly does pose a number of problems depending upon the degree of visual impairment, because it is, after all, a sighted world in which we live. And for the visually handicapped infant this means the social world. It has often been said that deafness cuts one off from people but that blindness only cuts one off from things. For the child or adult who becomes blind this may indeed be true, but for the child who is born blind, nothing could be further from the truth. Psychologists have long recognised that satisfactory adult relationships are largely dependent upon a satisfactory first relationship; and for the normal infant this means the mother or primary care-giver. The almost exclusive attention paid to mother-infant bonding in early ethological research certainly neglected the fact that other relationships are important, but anyone who has worked with the parents of a blind infant will attest to the importance of mutual attraction in maintaining behaviours which are taken for granted in the sighted, but which may fail to develop in the parents of the blind infant, with disastrous consequences for its later development.

Many mothers of sighted infants will say that their first feelings of love came when their infant looked at them, or when the infant gave its first smile. Of course, mothers may read into such responses more than is warranted, but these behaviours serve to keep them in close contact with their offspring, and

usually to make the whole arduous business of mothering a satisfying and rewarding experience. In the case of the infant who is born blind, these early precursors of bonding may well be absent, or severely limited in comparison with the sighted infant. If the infant cannot see, then how can it look? If its eyes are deformed or absent, then how can the mother bear to look at it? If the infant cannot see its mother's face, then how can it be expected to smile at the mother? In other words, how can the blind infant woo the mother into caring for it in the way the sighted infant does?

Fraiberg (1968) has described how the mother must be helped to recognise that her blind infant is responding to her presence in a number of subtle and unique ways, and she has emphasised the importance of the family therapist in acting as skilled intermediary between the blind infant and the natural care-giver. Because the blind infant has a more restricted repertoire of behaviours which are not instinctively interpreted by the parent, those subtle signs that do exist must be pointed out and built upon if the mother is not to end up feeling rejected by her infant, and in turn rejecting the infant herself. For example, a blind child's face often appears passive and uninterested, even when the mother is working hard to interact with him. Yet skilled observers are able to see that the child's hands are quite animatedly responding to the mother's voice. Mothers feel enormously elated when it is pointed out that the child has, in fact, been responding to them, only they had missed the signs, and they begin to take a much greater interest in the child. Similarly, if it can be demonstrated that the infant will smile only to the mother's voice and not to anyone else's, then she will recognise how special she is to her child. In other words, acceptance of the infant is often the first hurdle to be overcome.

The dangerous spiral of mutual withdrawal which can take place between even the best adjusted mother and her blind infant can be prevented only by expert counselling and family therapy, preferably from a developmental psychologist. Unfortunately, there are too few experienced workers around to do full justice to the complexities of the fragile but all-important mother-infant relationship, and things can often go badly wrong before the problem is identified. The parents themselves, still in a state of emotional turmoil, are unlikely to volunteer that not only have they failed to produce the normal baby which they expected, but that they are further failing to relate to it satisfactorily. The doctor, social worker, health visitor, or whoever, must be vigilant to the possibility that the infant is being rejected; a family with a blind infant is a family very much at risk, and one which needs expert support and intervention on a number of levels.

On the developmental side, it is important that the mother recognises that the development of a blind infant is different from that of a sighted one. Certain behaviours, such as those concerned with locomotion, emerge much later than they do in the sighted, and others, like crawling, may not occur at all. Language development may also appear to be retarded, and the young child may appear to be parroting the speech of others rather than using language in a creative fashion. These are typical behaviours, and parents should be reassured if they feel that their blind infant is developing differently from a sighted sibling in the family. At the same time, however, one should be aware that there can be sticking points for any developing infant, and in this respect the blind infant is even more liable to fail to move on to a new level of development. Only too often does one see a blind child who shows no social responsiveness, and who may exhibit autistic features such as rocking, head-banging, echolalia and eye-poking. Once established, these behaviours can be difficult to eradicate in later years, and they form an often impenetrable barrier to education and the whole process of socialisation.

*Problems of Referral*

In order that appropriate support can be given to the family, and given at the appropriate time, it is essential that the visually handicapped infant be identified at the earliest opportunity. Yet it is precisely here where many of the later problems have their origin. For example, the paediatrician may not pick up the more subtle signs of visual disorder unless he particularly expects one. Even if he does, there is no guarantee that he will immediately or automatically refer the infant to an ophthalmologist as opposed to adopting a philosophy of 'wait and see how things develop over the next few months'. Such a (common) response has cost an infant's life on more than one occasion, because, as we have seen in the case of an eye tumour, early removal is of the utmost importance. Other professionals, such as health visitors, who are trained to administer simple tests for squint or acuity problems, may in practice fail to carry out the test properly or appreciate what the results mean. Or the GP may resent being told by a paramedic that there is a suspected visual handicap.

The likely outcome of these failures in the referral system is that the infant with a visual handicap will fail to benefit from any medical intervention which may be currently available, and will grow up with an unnecessary handicap. Two common examples come to mind. Although total blindness is itself very rare, it has been estimated that about 1.5 per cent of the UK population suffer from uncorrected squint resulting in functional blindness in the squinting eye. If squint is identified early enough, surgical intervention can be almost completely successful. If, on the other hand, a squint is left uncorrected for several months, then no amount of surgical correction will enable the individual to have proper binocular vision after the age of around one year. Nor should the magnitude of the problem be underestimated. Research has shown that if squint and refractive errors are taken together, more children have defective vision than any other condition apart from dental disease. If these were reliably identified by the child's first birthday, then they could be virtually eradicated from the population. This remains one of the challenges of the future; but again, the source of the problem lies in the inadequacies of the referral system rather than of medical technology. It is an indictment of the system that an estimated 60 per cent of referrals can be attributable to lay sources, as opposed to only 40 per cent from medical and paramedical ones, and it is to be hoped that Area Health Authorities will come to recognise just how inadequate and fragmentary their services to the families of the visually handicapped can be. Among health visitors there is a strong feeling that there should be a specialist worker who can liaise directly with the hospital, or that a community-based ophthalmic clinic should be established, both alternatives eliminating the necessity of referral through a GP, and thus avoiding delay.

## Educational Provision

In spite of the desirability of early identification and the trend towards early registration, it is still not uncommon to find that many children are not registered as visually handicapped until just before they attain school age. Severe visual handicap denies the child access to the printed page and the blackboard, and the question therefore arises: should the child go to a school for the visually handicapped with the danger of becoming conditioned into the 'blindness system', or should he attend the local sighted school? Very often it is difficult to get a clear-cut answer to this question, and many individuals fall victim to an incorrect educational decision. The Vernon Report (DES, 1972) recommended that the goal should be to integrate the visually handicapped child into the sighted world, and expressed the desirability of giving special support to the child in a sighted school. However, it is one thing to agree upon a philosophy of education, but quite another to implement it. As Jamieson, Partlett and Pocklington (1977) point out, the debate on integration 'represents a tangled configuration of related arguments that draw together questions about virtually every aspect of how visually handicapped children should be educated'. Nor should one conclude that there is only one form of integration under consideration. The eventual form of integration decided upon at local level will clearly depend upon such factors as existing provision, prevalence of visual impairment locally, local authority policy, availability of specialist advisors and the existence of supplementary support. In other words, practicalities will be the ultimate determinants of the educational fate of any individual child.

The traditional alternative to integrated education is attendance, usually on a weekly residential basis, at a school for the blind or partially sighted, where all the relevant expertise and resources are available. The price to pay, however, is that the child will have to forego the many aspects of family life which most of us (unless we attended boarding school ourselves) take for granted. Often the school is situated at a considerable distance from home, so that valuable educational time is taken up in travel. But more importantly, the visually handicapped child will be spending more of his time in the company of other similarly or even more handicapped children than in the company of normally sighted peers, including siblings. Many educationalists see this as the most negative aspect of special schooling, and one which has the most lasting effect upon the individual.

Whatever the merits of integrated versus special education, in practice the decision is often made surprisingly easily. In some cases the practicalities prevent integration, whether these are constraints presented by local policy or lack of resources, or whether they are simply a reflection of the parents' attitude towards the child. In spite of all the support that parents may have received, not all parents feel that they can cope with the responsibility and strain of bringing up a blind child on a daily basis. In such cases it is probably better all round that the child be moved, at least for some of the time. Also, sighted brothers and sisters in a family may be neglected or made to feel that they must help the handicapped child at all times. This can bring about tensions and unhappiness within the family unit, and removing the visually handicapped child from the situation for periods of time can be beneficial. With a weekly boarding arrangement the family can have a relatively normal lifestyle during the week, but at the same time can adjust to a different type of social interaction at the weekend.

## Mobility Training

The education of the visually handicapped child, and in particular that of the blind child, must go far beyond providing literacy and numeracy by means of Braille, but must include training in posture, locomotion, orientation and navigation skills which the sighted take for granted. These various skills are collectively known as 'mobility', and mobility training comprises a considerable part of the blind child's educational experience. Here again, however, there is no consensus of opinion as to when formal mobility training should begin. This means that one child may receive mobility training from the first day at school, whereas another may have to wait a number of years before being introduced to a formal system of training, although all children will receive instruction in getting around the school in a way which is safe and which causes others the least inconvenience.

It is important to distinguish between formal mobility training and activities that encourage movement, body awareness and motor development. Formal mobility training consists of learning a range of specific skills which centre upon the use of the long cane, the guide cane or the guide dog. Guide dogs are not available as mobility aids for children, and the long cane is considered to be more suitable, although it renders the user somewhat conspicuous. Some children, in particular adolescent girls, prefer to use the shorter guide cane which permits them to move in a more natural manner, although it is not as efficient an aid as the long cane. The cane itself is best thought of as an extension of the hand which can be used to probe the ground ahead by means of regular scanning movements. As an aid to mobility, it is probably the most cost-effective, but training must be carried out by a qualified instructor. Every school for the blind has a Mobility Officer who can give training to any blind child unable to get about by sighted means.

Informal acquisition of movement skills, on the other hand, is something to be encouraged from the outset in the developing blind child, and this is best achieved through playing games which involve such activities as climbing, balancing, bouncing, swinging and the like. Those activities not only promote a sense of confidence and self-control, they also serve as a basis for social inter-action and parental involvement, as well as offering the child novel experiences which would otherwise be self-initiated. Tooze (1981) has suggested that parents should themselves try to learn what the world is like from the blind child's point of view, and she recommends that they wear a blindfold and try to identify and locate various sound sources in the home and immediate environ-ment. In this way they can come to understand that sounds can reliably inform one quite a lot about what is happening.

One mistake that some parents and even rehabilitators can make is that of assuming that because the blind infant has been deprived of one of his senses, all one has to do is to give massive stimulation through his remaining ones. Whilst sensory enrichment is certainly desirable, it should be applied intelli-gently and with structure if the child is to make any sense of it. There is nothing to be gained, for example, by leaving the radio or television set on

constantly in the belief that the child will somehow benefit from this passive experience. On the contrary, it is more likely that such background noise will interfere with the child's ability to listen to sounds which are meaningful in the context of his environment. Tooze recommends that mothers of blind infants and children carry them about the house as they go about their work, talking about what the various sounds produced mean in terms of activities that cannot be directly participated in; and her book has many other practical suggestions for helping a visually handicapped child come to terms with his world.

## Technological Solutions

In an age of increasing dependence on technology it is not surprising that various devices have been invented in an attempt to alleviate some of the problems of visual handicap, whether this be blindness or partial sight. The two main areas in which there have been significant technological advances are in the fields of communication and mobility. Over the past decade many children who would formerly have been educated by means of Braille have been able to benefit from sighted methods by the introduction of closed-circuit television systems (CCTV), which permit the magnification of print beyond that attainable using optical magnification. This means that even a legally blind child can learn by sighted methods. For those who possess no useful vision, micro-computer technology has enabled the storage and retrieval of information, which would formerly have been restricted to the bulky and inconvenient Braille system, on magnetic tape or disc. In this way the individual may gain rapid access to educational or even occupational material, and can quickly and effortlessly edit stored material. Such devices, although expensive, can open up new horizons in employment for the blind, and can make courses in computing available to the blind for the first time.

Whilst the inroads of microcomputer technology into communication for the blind have been considerable, the impact which it has had on mobility has regrettably been less impressive. This is not so much due to a lack of interest or inventiveness as to the nature of providing through touch or hearing the information which is sufficient to ensure safe travel. A number of ultrasonic devices, based on an understanding of bat navigation, have been produced over the last two decades, with the aim of providing the blind traveller with some sort of preview of his environment. In spite of much initial optimism, experience has shown that such devices are unable to replace the long cane or guide dog. They have therefore been relegated to the role of 'secondary aids'. The main reason for this is that, whereas bats and subaquatic mammals which navigate successfully using ultrasound can transcend the forces of gravity, man is constrained to creep about the earth's surface. This means that irregularities in the terrain must be picked up in advance. Unfortunately, ultrasound cannot reliably pick up this essential information. In addition, ultrasound tends to be reflected away from surfaces rather than back towards the aid, so that when there is an obstacle present the aid will not respond. This is most off-putting to the user, and is one reason for the lack of acceptance of such devices.

It is only recently that attention has been turned away from person-oriented technology to environment-oriented technology. One of the problems en-countered when attempting to modify the environment for one particular handicapped group is that the interests of the other groups may conflict. An example of such conflict concerns the introduction of tactile paving slabs to indicate the presence of Pelican crossings to the blind. Experimental trials indicated that certain patterns were unacceptable to wheel-chair users and those who had suffered from a stroke. Only after joint consultation was a mutually acceptable pattern agreed upon. On the other hand, adaptation of the environment for the visually handicapped may stand a better chance of being implemented if benefits are seen to accrue to the rest of the population rather than to one minority group. An example where this may be possible concerns the use of a voice-chip and a transponder which together can signal the impending arrival of a bus at a bus stop. On pushing a button, the user will be able to listen to a talking timetable, as well as being updated as to the number and destination of any bus approaching the stop. Such a facility, if it proves practicable, could have universal benefit.

These examples represent only a tiny proportion of the research effort currently being devoted to the problems of visually handicapped children and adults. What every blind person wants from technology, of course, is replacement vision, but in all honesty one must concede that we are still as far from that ideal as we were 20 years ago. It is not so much a problem of technological ignorance as one of a lack of understanding of how the visual system works, or how well other senses can use information artificially displayed to them. Some research scientists have experimented with an adapted ultrasonic mobility aid in an attempt to capitalise on what they see as the plasticity of the infant's perceptual system. They see the aid as a sensory surrogate which will enable the blind infant to develop along more normal sighted lines. To date, results of preliminary studies suggest that if the infant is under one year of age then benefits can be observed, but that after the first year, the infant does not accept the device so readily. These results seem to agree well with the other findings on early intervention.

In this necessarily brief account of visual handicap we have seen the enormous diversity of visual conditions which can affect the child and which can determine the sort of adult he or she becomes. We have also looked at the problems of referral and early diagnosis upon which successful intervention, whether medical, psychological or social, so crucially depends. We have also noted that the type of education to which we ultimately commit the blind child is likely to be determined more by local exigencies than any coherent educational philosophy.

An infant who is born blind is the one who stands the greatest risk of becoming ineducable, autistic, retarded in language development, and whose life is more likely to be lived out in an institution that in the family unit. We owe it to those blind infants of the future not to be complacent about existing health, social and educational provision. If we possess the relevant professional expertise it is our moral duty to champion the cause of the visually handicapped, however uncomfortable that may be for the *status quo*. To do less would be to do them a disservice.

## Further Reading

Chapman, E.K. (1978) *Visually Handicapped Children and Young People*, Special Needs in Education Series, London: Routledge & Kegan Paul

Dobree, J.H. and Boulter, E. (1982) *Blindness and Visual Handicap: The Facts*, Oxford University Press

Fraiberg, S. (1977) *Insights from the Blind*, Human Horizons Series, London: Souvenir Press

Tooze, D. (1981) *Independence Training for Visually Handicapped Children*, Croom Helm Special Education Series, London: Croom Helm

Warren, D. (1977) *Blindness and Early Childhood Development*, New York: American Foundation for the Blind, Inc.

# CHAPTER 5

# Cerebral Palsy

BILL GILLHAM

## The Nature of the Condition

The popular term for cerebral palsy is 'spastic' (as in 'The Spastics Society'), but the spastic type is just one form of cerebral palsy, although the predominant one. However, the term 'cerebral palsy' is itself inadequate because, apart from having a curiously old-fashioned ring, it covers an enormous range of conditions, the common factor being some lesion of the brain or abnormality of brain growth, affecting the motor function.

The description is usually reserved for damage acquired during the stage when the brain is developing rapidly. Commonly, this damage occurs *perinatally* — for example due to severe anoxia at birth. But the damage can occur prenatally or during the first two or three years of life.

Cerebral palsy is quite distinct from spina bifida (see Chapter 7), even though the affected children may be similarly wheelchair bound. The difference is in the main *site of the lesion*: primarily in the *spinal cord* in spina bifida (although a brain lesion due to hydrocephalus is usually also evident); primarily in the *brain* (cerebrum or cerebellum) in the case of the child with cerebral palsy. The approximate site of the lesion, and its related effects in terms of motor dysfunction, is the major source of diagnostic classification in cerebral palsy. But it has to be said that medical authorities are far from being in complete agreement with each other; indeed, no two writers on the subject adopt a descriptive system which is identical even on major details.

The disagreement is not so much an academic dispute but rather a reflection of the complexity of the disabilities resulting from brain injury. Consider the side-view illustration of the brain (left cerebral hemisphere) which shows the main, approximately localised, functional areas (Figure 5.1).

Brain injury is rarely discriminating: damage to the motor area is likely to be accompanied by damage to other areas. At the same time the relationship between extent of brain damage and loss of function is far from simple. Extensive brain damage can result in minimal loss of function; the reverse is also true. What is more we all have *two* brains: two hemispheres, superficially identical, which control the contra-lateral (opposite) sides of the body, but which can 'share' certain functions in response to injury, though not including those of motor control.

The commonest form of cerebral palsy is *hemiplegia*, where only one side of

*Figure 5.1: The Left Cerebral Hemisphere of the Brain*

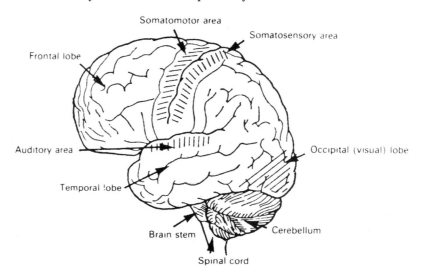

the body is affected. We are most familiar with this in those who have suffered from a stroke, and this is, in fact, one way of understanding what hemiplegia involves. Hemiplegia may be very mild in character and scarcely detectable without specialist examination, especially when it affects the *sub-dominant* side of the body, i.e. our non-preferred hand and foot, which we accept as having inferior function.

But even if the cerebrum is undamaged, some of the most serious conditions, e.g. ataxia (see later) can arise from damage to the cerebellum, which has a kind of exchange-control function in the central nervous system, i.e. it directs where 'messages' are sent in the brain.

In cerebral palsy the lesion is usually 'non-progressive': in other words it doesn't get any better or any worse; but, of course, it occurs in a growing and developing child so that the visible condition can change, for better or worse.

Many kinds of cerebral palsy are difficult to detect or, at least, diagnostically differentiate in the first few months of life. As with many other handicapping conditions it is often the parents who first notice that something is wrong; for example, unusual balancing movements in attempting to walk, dragging of the legs in crawling. But even when detected, the prognosis of the ultimate disability can rarely be made with absolute confidence — much to the disgust of the parents! However, professional judgement is not to be confused with apparent confidence of professional pronouncements. We are still largely ignorant of the working of the brain, more so of the damaged brain: the latter is not just a brain with a bit missing, but a reorganised brain, working to its own rules.

The complexity and uncertainty surrounding cerebral palsy have been outlined in order that the following, necessarily simplified, descriptive account is seen as a great deal tidier than the reality.

**Types of Cerebral Palsy**

The three main types of cerebral palsy are:

*spastic* — the condition most people would recognise as cerebral palsy, with heightened muscle tone leading to 'clasp-knife' type movements, exaggerated reflexes and lack of muscular strength;
*athetosis* — successive, almost continuous writhing movements of the limbs, most in evidence when the child attempts to grasp something;
*ataxia* — most apparent when the child is attempting to walk: uncoordinated, widespread gait with marked tremor and head movement.

'Mixed' conditions are common, especially when the handicap is severe.

*Spastic Cerebral Palsy*

As mentioned earlier, *hemiplegia*, although the commonest, is the most difficult to detect early, especially in its milder forms. It may not be apparent until those age-levels when the main stages of motor development are achieved — sitting, standing and walking. The more severe the condition, the earlier and the more easily it is diagnosed; but a very mild condition may not be detected until school age, when clumsiness and poor fine hand control may be noted by the child's teachers.

Brain injury always brings with it an increased risk of epilepsy, and this is the case with hemiplegia, the risk being correlated with the seriousness of the condition — around 50 per cent in the case of the severely hemiplegic.

Retrospectively, it has to be assumed that there was some perinatal or prenatal abnormality for hemiplegia to have occurred. But the history of the birth and pregnancy typically reveals only minor abnormalities, characteristic of the birth history of many perfectly normal babies.

*Diplegia* is an impairment of function of all four limbs but primarily the legs. (*Paraplegia* — involvement of the legs only — is not a form of cerebral palsy, being the result of a spinal lesion. *Quadriplegia*, the approximately equal involvement of all four limbs, is less common than diplegia.

Perhaps because diplegia is the outcome of more extensive damage than hemiplegia there is a much stronger link with abnormalities of pregnancy and birth — especially prematurity. Improvements in perinatal care appear to have reduced the incidence of spastic diplegia, but birth difficulties are only one cause and so the scope for further improvement is limited.

*Athetosis*

Athetosis shows itself in rapid fluctuations of muscle tone which results in facial contortions and grimaces, and writhing movements of the limbs, especially when the child is excited or making an effort to do something. When asleep the movements disappear entirely. The main cause is severe perinatal anoxia and, in the past, neonatal jaundice.

## *Ataxia*

Ataxia is related to abnormalities of the cerebellum resulting in general developmental delay and abnormal movement patterns which include a prolongation of the unsteady, broadly based walk of the toddler. There is a wide variation in the incidence of ataxia cited by different authorities due partly, perhaps, to problems of diagnosis, but also to variations between different populations due to familial, genetic factors. Most cases where diagnosis is unequivocal are probably prenatal in origin, although postnatal infections such as meningitis can also lead to a cerebellar lesion.

## *Incidence of Cerebral Palsy*

Wide variations in incidence are reported internationally, particularly within diagnostic categories. Apart from 'real' incidence, the available data undoubtedly vary according to diagnostic judgement and related screening procedures. Incidence in the UK is approximately the same as for spina bifida — about 1 in 350 births. There does appear to have been a significant decline in incidence, presumably because of improvements in prenatal and perinatal care and the treatment and prevention of such diseases as neonatal jaundice; but gains here have been counterbalanced by the improved care of premature and other 'at risk' babies, with the result that more damaged babies have survived.

## Associated Disabilities

It must be repeated that the foregoing descriptive account is both simpler and tidier than the actual clinical manifestations of the condition. It has already been mentioned that cerebral palsy is often of a mixed type, though with one type predominant. But cerebral palsy, especially if it is severe, is *normally* associated with other significant handicaps — as covered by other chapters in the present book. In part this is obvious: functions such as speech and vision depend upon fine control of complex muscle systems; in particular is this true of speech. Quite small impairments here can disrupt the fine co-ordinations involved. Thus, it is not surprising that around half of the children with cerebral palsy have no speech or a significant speech defect. Perhaps 20 per cent have a significant visual defect, and approximately the same proportion a significant hearing loss (which interacts with their expressive language difficulties). Estimates of epilepsy vary, partly according to diagnostic category, but it probably occurs in at least 25 per cent of cases.

Intellectual development — a term, it must be remembered, which covers a complex range of abilities — is commonly severely affected. It is easy to underestimate the ability of a child with little speech and a conspicuous physical disability, but the assumption that in cerebral palsy a normal intelligence is trapped inside a defective body is certainly a myth. But *sometimes* a child with a severe condition manifests evidence of a very superior intelligence even though this is against the trend of the effects. Brain damage is the major cause of severe and profound mental handicap; and it is not usually discriminating.

As might be expected, the degree of mental handicap generally varies with the severity of the cerebral palsy. Spastic hemiplegia has a lesser implication for impaired general intellectual functioning, on average, although specific learning disabilities, e.g. with reading, are common: this is probably related to the site of the damage and in which hemisphere it occurs. In cases of spastic diplegia, and especially spastic quadriplegia, mental retardation is both more common and typically more severe. However, it must be repeated, superior intelligence can be found in a child with a severe form of spastic diplegia. Athetosis is quite often associated with near-normal intelligence; ataxia is the most likely to be associated with severe mental handicap.

## A Multi-disciplinary Approach

The formidable (and conspicuous) problems faced by a child with cerebral palsy, and his caretakers, brought about one of the first large-scale parent-initiated helping organisations in the UK — The Spastics Society, founded 1952. The 1950s and 1960s were decades of great optimism about improved methods of treatment, and the role that medical research would play in this process. Important progress was made at that time but had reached a plateau by the early 1970s, and it can now be seen that the expectations of that period were unrealistic. Certainly, during the past decade there have been few noteworthy advances in the treatment of cerebral palsy, at least from a medical point of view. Indeed, the initiative for development appears to have passed from medicine to psychology and special education.

It is likely that most parents have always been more realistic than some professionals. And, for their part, professionals are now more alive to the need for a multi-disciplinary approach to the problems of the multiply handicapped, cerebrally palsied child. For the parents it is an awesome responsibility, and their main need *from the beginning* is for co-ordinated professional advice, essentially practical in character. This should include:

— medical surveillance, preferably by a paediatrician who knows the child and family well and can co-ordinate the contribution of other medical specialists;
— physiotherapy advice to the parents on handling to encourage development and avoid the problems that come with growth and the child's attempts to use his limbs;
— advice and help from the occupational therapist on practical problems of management;
— advice and help from a educational visitor or home teacher on the

development and monitoring of the child's abilities (preferably with the support of an educational psychologist);
— advice from a specialist speech therapist on the development of early language and prespeech forms of communication.

It has to be said that such a comprehensive range of services is not often available in terms of separate professional contributions. The most reliable help is likely to come from the physiotherapist and/or the occupational therapist. A good occupational therapist can provide a range of advice and practical help (see, for example, *Daily Living with the Handicapped Child* Diana Millard's book in the present series). 'Educational' help is also varied in its implications. In her book *Toys and Play for the Handicapped Child*, also in the present series, Barbara Riddick describes the use of toys and play for developing motor skills and co-ordination, as well as those which encourage cognitive skills.

*Systems of Physiotherapy*

There are numerous systems of physiotherapy treatment for children with cerebral palsy, some of which make or imply dramatic claims for effectiveness although the theoretical basis may be doubtful and adequate evaluation lacking.

The neurodevelopmental therapy devised by K. and B. Bobath is the most widely used programme internationally. In the UK the Bobaths' techniques have been developed by Nancy Finnie of Charing Cross Hospital into a form of therapy and management for parents to use at home. In physiotherapy, as in other regular forms of treatment, the effectiveness lies not so much in 'special-ist' sessions as in good 'normal' practice in the home. For example, how a child is picked up will encourage (or discourage) abnormal reflex patterns; regular changes of position (and the positions that are selected) will reduce risk of deformity or the development of undesirable patterns of movement.

Apparatus as simple as foam wedges can give the child a better position or one which offers a different view of the world. Standing frames will give a child the experience of being upright before he can walk — or if walking is impos-sible. (See illustrations on p. 73.)

Aids to walking, from special boots to walking frames, have much improved with the use of modern, lightweight materials. But selecting what is appropriate for a particular child is a matter of specialist advice.

If there is one simple aim in physiotherapy it is to enable the child to walk. Most cerebrally palsied children achieve this goal, at least to a limited degree. But walking that is adequate for moving around within the home environment is often not adequate for moving around in the outside world. Probably around half of cerebrally palsied children need the use of a wheelchair or something similar. The range is now enormous — from toy-type devices that can be hand-paddled or scooted, right up to sophisticated, electric self-propelled wheel-chairs with controls specially adapted to the manual limitations of a person with cerebral palsy.

## Management in Daily Living

In many respects it is impossible to distinguish between the contribution from physiotherapy and the contribution from occupational therapy: when trans-lated to the home environment they merge to a large extent. The occupational therapist also takes on an educational role, as does the speech therapist. Over-lap need not present problems for parents if there is good teamwork. Many practical problems in daily living follow from impairment of motor function. Advice on the handling and positioning of the child has to be worked out in detail, for example in relation to toileting and bathing arrangements.

A particular problem is that of feeding: the baby with cerebral palsy may be unable to suck so that feeding has to take place without his active co-operation. For a long time the child may have difficulty in swallowing, or he may choke or gag on his food. Regurgitation is also quite common. Most of these difficulties can be overcome, but they are particularly distressing to parents anxious to do their best for their child. Practical help (not just 'advice') in overcoming these problems is essential to relieve parental stress. The child's position when feed-ing, the atmosphere and setting of the feeding situation, the type and texture of foodstuffs, the amount given and the timing are examples of the variables that can be adjusted, and which are normally sufficient.

Because cerebral palsy is a conspicuous physical handicap, it is easy to think of it as a physical, almost mechanical problem. But much of any difficulty that arises lies in the parental handling of the child and the problems he presents.

The child's physical difficulties are always made much worse if he is upset or excited. Confident handling by the parents communicates itself to the child — as it does in all parent-child relationships — but with a handicapped child parents are less likely to be confident that they are doing the right thing, or may be anxious that they are being too hard on the child, and so on.

A common source of stress for parents, characteristic of other brain-injured children or those where such a diagnosis is suspected, is irregular or disturbed sleep. It has to be emphasised that this is a problem not so much for the child (who presumably gets what sleep he needs) but for the adults who have to look after him. Regular but unpredictable sleep disruption can rapidly bring otherwise stable parents to the point of breakdown. For that reason it may be the first problem to tackle. Psychological management techniques are often the most effective. Cerebrally palsied children quickly learn to 'manage' their parents in this way; and parents are more likely to give in to their handicapped child precisely because he is handicapped. It is, quite often, just an example of the problems of socialisation posed for handicapped children by adults who, out of sympathy, condition them to make unreasonable demands.

### Problems of Language and Communication

Speech is one of the most complex of our motor functions and is itself dependent on the quality of other functions, especially hearing. Problems of language and communication are the main handicaps allied to cerebral palsy. Quite often the cerebral palsy has to be regarded as the secondary handicap.

Speech and the numerous non-verbal aspects of communication — eye-contact, gesture, and so on — are fundamental to the development of social relations as well as intellectual abilities. Of course, parents make great efforts to understand their child's communicative intentions and are often amazingly skilful at interpreting minimal cues. But although most children manage to develop forms of communication that are adequate with those who know them well, they may still be gravely limited in a wider social context. And a minimum adequacy for social purposes will not be sufficient for educational progress which largely depends on the development of comprehension and expression in spoken and written language, *particularly the latter.*

The main language problem in children with cerebral palsy is lack of expressive language (speech) or severely disordered speech. *Comprehension* of speech, however, may be very good, depending largely on the degree of hearing impairment — and sometimes very good despite that. Comprehension of written language (reading) can often be achieved by children with poor speech, and sometimes this seems to improve spoken language; but since visual perceptual problems are common, progress can be limited. Expression of written language in the form of handwriting is often impossible or very difficult: and it is here, in particular, that  modern technology has come to the rescue.

The last decade has seen a great expansion in different forms of non-speech communication systems using signs or symbols (see Chapter 2). But apart from the limitations implicit in the systems themselves, e.g. restricted vocabulary and grammar, the intellectual difficulty of some of them, and lack of 'common currency' usefulness, they are often of limited value to children whose fine hand control is poor: and these are commonly the children who cannot achieve speech.

Since some children with severe cerebral palsy can be shown by specialised psychological testing to have superior non-verbal intellectual skills (of reasoning and levels of category construction), the technological challenge is a very real one. Fortunately, the technological revolution in microelectronics is more than just a copy-writer's cliché, and so we have a range of aids which can be interactive and/or adapted to the needs and abilities (especially the degree of voluntary control) of cerebrally palsied children. The 'Possum' typewriter (see illustration) has been with us for some time, but is a good simple example of the genre: using an adaptable joystick the child selects letters for typing from a large visual display. Electronic voice synthesisers incorporating a 'memory' for sentence construction can also be used via a variety of touch controls.

**Meeting Educational Needs**

Many children with cerebral palsy are capable of managing in normal schools with a modest amount of special help and special arrangements. With better

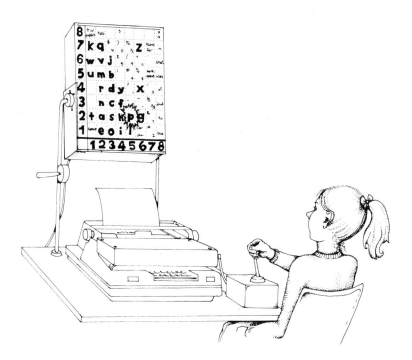

planning and provision the number could certainly be extended. But the range of handicaps which often come together in one child, and the need for special equipment means that a special school or unit is the only practicable way of meeting the child's needs. One estimate of the extent of cerebrally palsied children's disabilities is that, on average, they have two-and-a-half handicaps. A child with spastic diplegia may well be mentally handicapped and have a significant hearing loss: without very special teaching and facilities his chances of making progress are minimal.

Mental handicap is both more prevalent and more severe than in the case of spina bifida, for example, although the degree of motor handicap may be similar. Most studies agree that approximately 50 per cent of cerebrally palsied children are mildly to profoundly mentally handicapped. To this has to be added the correlated high incidence of problems of communication. When these are added to the basic problems of mobility and voluntary movement, we have to recognise that the achievements of these children are often remarkable.

In the 1950s and 1960s children with a severe condition quite commonly went to residential schools, many of which were set up by The Spastics Society. At that time local authority day provision was limited, and residential schools were often seen as centres of specialised excellence. But day provision has improved radically during the past 15-20 years, and the costs of residential schooling have increased astronomically. There have also been doubts about the wisdom of taking a young handicapped child away from his family, excellent though many residential schools undoubtedly are. Decisions about educational placement are not simple. Every case has to be considered on its merits and is not just a matter of the severity of the physical handicap: problems of communication and the degree of mental handicap are often more important in making a placement decision.

The 1980s seem to be the decade of realism about cerebral palsy as well as handicaps in general. If progress in medical management of the condition seems to have levelled off in the last 10-15 years, this is not to underestimate the contribution from medicine. However, we cannot change the fundamental condition at all and only modify its effects to a limited degree. What we can do is to develop adapted procedures which enable children with cerebral palsy to be as mobile as possible, to interact and communicate with others, to learn and develop their abilities. And, across all the professions, it has become clear that the major therapeutic resource is the child's parents, and that professional effectiveness is largely a function of effective collaboration with them.

## Further Reading

Finnie, N. (1974) *Helping the Young Cerebrally Palsied Child at Home* (2nd ed), London: Heinemann (Much more than a book about physiotherapy: a first-class practical manual.)
Newson, E. and Hipgrave, A. (1982) *Getting Through to Your Handicapped Child*, Cambridge:

Cambridge University Press (Particularly good on communication tactics.)
Russell, P. (1984) *The Wheelchair Child* (2nd ed), London: Souvenir Press (Not just about
cerebrally palsied children, but a practical and insightful book about the needs and problems
of children who are dependent on a wheelchair.)

## Information and advice can also be obtained from:

The Spastics Society
12 Park Crescent
London W1N 4EQ
Tel: 01 636 5020

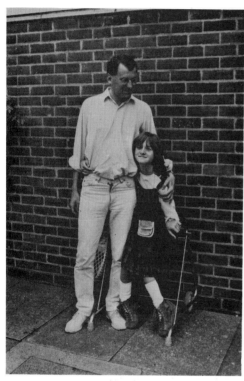 

# CHAPTER 6

# Epilepsy

RUTH GILLHAM

## The Condition

A standard text defines epilepsy as a

> symptom due to excessive temporary neuronal discharging which results from intracranial or extracranial causes: epilepsy is characterised by discrete episodes, which tend to be recurrent, in which there is a disturbance of movement, sensation, behaviour and/or consciousness.

The rest of this section is devoted to expanding and explaining this definition so that the nature of epilepsy, its causes and forms, become clear.

### 'Neuronal Discharging'

Nerve cells (neurons) are the means by which sensations are transmitted from the sense organs to the brain, and by which impulses from the brain are transmitted to muscles to initiate and control their movement. Within the brain, itself a mass of billions of neurons, there is a constant flow of nerve impulses as incoming messages are processed, plans are considered and put into action, and all the various aspects of intellect and emotion are carried on.

Neurons consist of a cell body, which is capable of forming connections with other similar cell bodies, and an axon, a major fibre which varies from one millimetre to one metre in length and serves to connect the cell body with receptors in muscle or sense organs. A diagrammatic representation of a neuron is shown in Figure 6.1.

Impulses are conducted along axons by means of alterations in concentration gradients of sodium and potassium ions across the cell membrane. Any basic biology or physiology text will explain this process in more detail, but the net effect is similar to that of an electric current passing along a wire. The 'excessive neuronal discharging' referred to in the definition is excessive activity in impulse conduction in a group of neurons. This abnormal activity can be contained within one part of the brain, giving rise to focal or partial seizures, or it can spread throughout the brain, giving rise to generalised seizures. It should be understood that it is not the electrical activity itself that is abnormal, since there is continual electrical activity in the brain, but its intensity, frequency and the way in which it propagates.

Although the excessive neuronal discharging which produces seizures is

74

*Figure 6.1: Diagrammatic Representation of a Neuron*

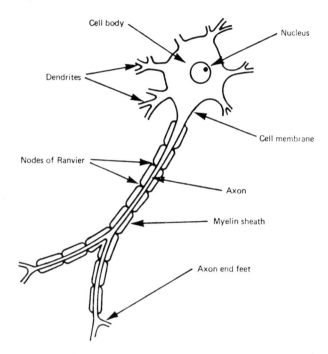

intermittent — each seizure is a separate event — there is usually some continual abnormal pattern of electrical activity in the brain of someone who has recurrent seizures. This can be recorded by electroencephalography (EEG) and the resulting traces play an important part in making a firm diagnosis of epilepsy.

## Causes of Epilepsy

Having established that a seizure is a burst of abnormal electrical activity in the brain, we need to examine why some people are prone to seizures and not others. In fact *anyone* can have an epileptic seizure given sufficient provocation. For example, withdrawal of alcohol after a heavy drinking bout may produce seizures in people not otherwise seizure prone. What separates those who can be said to suffer from epilepsy from those who do not, is the ease with which they have seizures. It is often not possible to establish exactly why the brain of any particular individual should have a low threshold for seizure activity. The condition may be present from birth, or the brain may be left hyperexcitable and seizure prone after an infective illness. Sometimes seizure activity begins in old age and is related to the rapid degeneration of brain tissue in senile dementia.

There may be a particular area of the brain which has become electrically unstable and gives bursts of seizure activity. In this case there is invariably an underlying lesion. It may be scar tissue caused by a head injury or by a neurosurgical operation. The lesion may be a tumour, an abnormal blood vessel or an area of damage caused by an interruption in blood supply.

*Causes of Seizures*

Even when the reason for an individual's seizure proneness is known, the question of why he should have a seizure at one particular moment and not at another remains unanswered. There are neurophysiological explanations of how a group of neurons become increasingly unstable until there is a spontaneous discharge of excessive activity, but it is also known that seizures can occur in response to some particular external or internal stimulus. Some indication of the wide variety of factors which may trigger seizures in individuals sensitive to them are listed below.

Psychological factors: Anxiety
Excitement
Anger
Anticipation
Surprise
Physiological states:  Fatigue
Inactivity/drowsiness
Hormonal changes, e.g. menstruation, pregnancy
Fever
Over hydration
Hyperventilation
Anoxia
Metabolic imbalances, e.g. hypoglycaemia,
hypocalcaemia
Toxic states
Drug or alcohol withdrawal
Sensory factors:  Particular light frequencies
Particular visual patterns
Particular sounds
Touch to particular areas of skin

These factors vary enormously in their influence. For example, most people will have a seizure in response to withdrawal of some drugs if they have taken enough over a longish period. On the other hand, sensitivity to particular sensory stimulation is rare. Any epileptic individual may be sensitive to several of these factors working together, to only one, or to none of these. Most patients have theories about what brings on an attack, but these may not always be confirmed by observation and investigation.

*Types of Seizure*

The definition at the head of this section referred to 'disturbance of movement, sensation, behaviour and/or consciousness'. A description of the observable manifestations of the various types of seizure will make the nature of these disturbances more clear.

Current terminology divides seizures into two categories: generalised and partial. Basically the former involves the whole brain and the latter only part. Among *generalised seizures* are 'absences' or *petit mal*, most commonly seen in children. There is a brief loss of awareness during which facial expression remains fixed and body motionless. The individual will not speak or respond to speech. After the attack, which may only last for seconds, he may resume activity without being aware that anything has happened. These seizures are often very frequent, occurring ten to twenty times a day or more. Children suffering from these attacks may be misrepresented as day-dreamers or poor listeners.

'Tonic-clonic seizures', also known as *grand mal* or generalised convulsions, are sometimes preceded by a period of irritability and tension lasting for several hours or days. The usual course of this type of seizure is sudden loss of consciousness, with the patient becoming rigid and falling to the ground, some- times with a cry. He may urinate, and breathing may be briefly arrested. This tonic phase is followed by jerking of face, body and both arms and legs. These movements become less and disappear, leaving the person comatose. Consciousness slowly returns, but he may feel confused, unwell or drowsy for some time afterwards. Occasionally he may experience a great feeling of relief and well-being. Tonic-clonic seizures are very alarming to the observer, but provided the patient does not injure himself in falling there is usually no cause for continuing anxiety.

There are other variants of generalised seizures, but on the whole they contain some of the features of the above.

*Partial seizures* are a form of epilepsy where there is always a particular focus in the brain from which the epileptic activity arises. The seizure may remain partial or focal or it may lead to secondary generalised seizures, as described above. The symptoms of the seizure will depend on the site of the abnormal discharge. If it is in the motor cortex, twitching and jerking may occur in one group of muscles. The seizure may be confined to this area or may spread to include other areas on the same side of the body. Foci in other areas of the brain may provoke strange sensations or visual distortions, or sudden floods of emotion.

'Temporal lobe seizures' are the most common type of partial seizure and will therefore be described in a little more detail. It is probably no exaggeration to say that there are as many different types of temporal lobe seizure as there are patients with temporal lobe epilepsy. The attacks often begin with some kind of sensation. The patient may be quite unable to describe this, or it may be an hallucination of a taste or smell or commonly of an unpleasant feeling rising up from the stomach to the chest and throat. There may be visual distor- tions, such as objects looking small and far away, or auditory hallucinations.

There may be disturbance of memory so that the patient feels he is in a totally unfamiliar environment, or feels that an unfamiliar environment is familiar. Sometimes there is forced recall of particular phrases or scenes. There may be a feeling of fear, anxiety, ecstasy, grief or some other strong emotion. The person may carry out some activity, often coherent in itself but inappropriate to the situation. He might, for example, take off some item of clothing, or walk off in a random direction. An individual may experience some or none of these phenomena, but it is likely that for each individual each seizure is similar, sometimes indistinguishable from other seizures.

## Incidence

Most sources agree that the incidence of epilepsy is approximately 30 to 50 per 100,000 of population, with rates for males slightly higher than for females. The rate changes with age, being relatively high in the first year of life, falling throughout childhood and rising again over the age of 60.

Seizure types have different relative frequencies. In one series of 6,000 patients, 24 per cent had seizures which could not be classified. Of the remainder (where classification was possible) 38 per cent had some type of generalised seizure and 62 per cent some form of partial seizure.

## Assessment and Diagnosis

### Observation

The first step to a diagnosis of epilepsy is for a seizure to be observed. The medical practitioner concerned will require a reliable description from an eye witness.

*Before the Attack.*   If the patient has had any recent illness, accident or injury or emotional stress this should be reported, as it may give a clue to the nature of the attack. It is also important to describe events occurring immediately before the incident. The child's behaviour may have changed in some way. Some people become irritable and aggressive, or, if they feel some warning of an attack, quiet and withdrawn. Something may have happened immediately before the attack to provoke it. The child may have been crying and hyperventilating, for example, or staring fixedly at a visual pattern. If there have been any previous similar occurrences these should also be described.

*During the Attack.*   The course of the attack should be described as exactly as possible so that it is known whether or not the child fell, whether or not he injured himself, was incontinent of urine or faeces, whether he bit his tongue, whether there were any twitching and jerking movements and, if so, where. It should also be noted whether the child spoke, or responded to speech or other external stimuli. The length of time from onset to return to normal should be reported.

*After the Attack.* It is helpful if the child's recovery is described, including details of his behaviour, whether or not he was confused, complained of headache, was drowsy, and whether he knew what had happened.

The relevance of most of these points can be seen with reference to the description of seizure types. A good description may not only give the physician an idea of whether the attack is epileptic, but also of the type of epilepsy. In any case, he will wish to exclude any illness which may have caused the attack and which requires treatment. For example, the seizures may have occurred in the context of a febrile illness. They may have occurred shortly after a blow to the head, in which case further investigation of the head injury becomes a priority.

Assuming that there is no underlying illness which requires urgent treatment, the physician may start some drug treatment straight away, or he may refer the child for an EEG. This will depend on the precise circumstances of the case.

## EEG

Transmission of impulses and signals in the brain is by means of electrical conduction along nerve cells, and across junctions between cells. Electrical activity in the brain can be picked up by electrodes attached to the surface of the scalp. Conductivity is increased by placing a blob of salt-gel between the electrode and the skin. The process is quite painless. Changes in voltage occurring in the brain are picked up by the electrodes, greatly amplified, and recorded by styluses on moving paper as a series of traces (Figure 6.2).

Although useful, an EEG only gives information about activity in some parts of the brain at the time of recording. It is possible to have epilepsy and an EEG which appears normal. It is also possible to have an abnormal EEG but to have no neurological illness. In the case of children in particular, it may be difficult to get the co-operation required to obtain a good recording. It is important to remain still and relaxed, otherwise the trace is obscured by movement artefact.

Sometimes, however, it may be possible to record activity which is clearly abnormal and which has the typical pattern of epileptic discharge. If doubt as to the nature of the attacks remains there are more specialised EEG techniques available; for example, monitoring the EEG for prolonged periods while the child is walking about and carrying out normal activities. The record is stored on a cassette, and if he has a seizure that part of the trace can be played back and examined in detail.

## Non-epileptic Attacks

There are a number of conditions which may produce attacks, some of which appear similar to seizures. In childhood, breath-holding, hyperventilating, temper-tantrums and faints are all sometimes confused with epileptic attacks.

*Figure 6.2: Partial Epilepsy: EEG Trace of 10-year-old Child with Temporal Lobe Epilepsy, Probably Due to Birth Trauma*

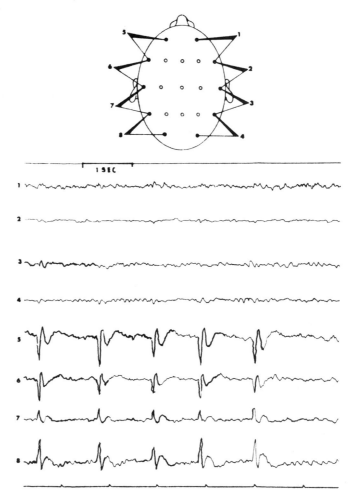

Source: Reproduced from J.M. Sutherland and M.J. Eadie (1980) *The Epilepsies: Modern Diagnosis and Treatment.*

There are, of course, serious conditions which may cause the child to collapse and become unconscious, but unlike the aforementioned these are unlikely to be brief and to be followed by rapid spontaneous recovery, and therefore less likely to be confused with seizures. Many children who have epilepsy also have non-epileptic seizures. These may occur because a child imagines he is going to have a seizure, because he has something to gain by having one, or for any other psychological reason. Non-epileptic seizures also occur in people who do not have epilepsy. If they have witnessed a seizure these attacks may be very difficult to distinguish.

Good descriptions of attacks can help the physician decide whether they are likely to be epileptic, but sometimes the question is not resolved. As previously noted, EEGs are helpful but can never provide absolutely conclusive evidence that an attack which occurred at a time other than during recording was epileptic. The physician needs to judge carefully on the balance of the evidence because he has to determine the appropriate treatment. For other people involved in the day-to-day management of the child the distinction is not so important. It is unwise for the layman to make judgements about what is and what is not a 'genuine' seizure. As far as he is concerned, the general rules for management apply in any case. This point will be expanded in a later section.

In summary then, in order to make a firm diagnosis the physician would like to have:

(i)  clear descriptions of several attacks which conform to one or other forms of epilepsy;
(ii)  an EEG which shows seizure activity;
(iii)  a good response to treatment with anti-convulsant drugs.

It is usually possible to establish these criteria, but occasionally it may take some time or may never be entirely or satisfactorily resolved.

## Management of Seizures

### 'First Aid'

The following points are intended for the guidance of people who are responsible for a child liable to seizures:

1. Prevent him from injuring himself if he falls or thrashes about, but touch him as little as possible.
2. Do not try to hold him down.
3. Never put anything in his mouth.
4. Prevent a crowd from gathering.
5. If he falls asleep immediately after the seizure, leave him on his side until he wakes.
6. Allow time for full recovery. Some people are confused or easily alarmed soon after a seizure.
7. Normal activity should be resumed after he has recovered from the attack. Children should not be sent home from school unless absolutely necessary.
8. Avoid fuss: too much attention may either cause social embarrassment or may be rewarding and increase the likelihood of further attacks.
9. Medical attention is not required unless:

(a)  it is the child's first seizure;
(b)  he requires treatment for an injury sustained during the attack;

(c) the seizure is unduly prolonged or is followed by others in rapid succession.

An 'unduly prolonged seizure' is a little difficult to define, but in most cases the actual seizure lasts only for a few minutes. The drowsiness which sometimes follows may last for an hour or more.

### Drug Treatments

Assuming that there is no underlying treatable disease or condition, the most reliable and practical method of controlling epileptic seizures is with anticonvulsant medication. There is a wide variety of drugs available, some more suited for some forms of attack, and some others. In general, they work by increasing the threshold at which the abnormal activity in the brain will occur. Normal practice is to start the child on one drug in a low dosage and increase it until the seizures are controlled without overdosing. Sometimes it is necessary to change from one drug to another or take two or more different ones at the same time before satisfactory control is achieved. A few individuals continue to have frequent seizures despite numerous trials of drug combinations. Sometimes other treatments (described below) can help people with poorly controlled seizures.

The following guidelines apply to people responsible for the day-to-day administration of drugs to an epileptic child:

1. Never increase or decrease dosage without instructions from the child's doctor.

2. Never discontinue drugs because they don't seem to be doing any good, or because the child has had no seizures for a long time.

3. If the child complains of dizziness, poor balance, blurred or double vision or is unduly sleepy, he may be on too high a dosage. Consult his doctor without delay, but do not change the dosage yourself.

4. Make sure the child is actually taking his tablets, and not hiding them or spitting them out.

5. As soon as he is able, get him to take responsibility for taking his pills. Getting the habit established under supervision will help prevent him forgetting when he is old enough to be independent.

6. It is important to take the drugs at the same time every day. This establishes a routine which is hard to forget and keeps the level of drug in the blood reasonably constant. A long delay between dosages, particularly for drugs with a shorter half-life, may cause a drop in blood level and the emergence of seizure activity.

### Surgery

Occasionally surgical operations are carried out for the relief of seizures, but these are only done under certain conditions. If the seizure activity is arising from a tumour or an abnormal collection of blood vessels, it may be possible to remove this. The feasibility of such an operation will depend on the size and site of the lesion, whether or not it is likely to get bigger and how much of a problem it is causing, both in terms of seizure frequency and other neurological symptoms. The operation itself will cause scar tissue to form and this may give rise to further seizures, or there may be a complete cessation of seizure activity. The risks and outcome naturally vary according to the features of each individual case.

Sometimes a lobe of the brain is removed completely if it contains an epileptogenic focus. This is usually one or other of the temporal lobes (see Figure 5.1) but frontal lobes are also occasionally removed. Such an operation is only done if it can be established with certainty that the part of the brain for removal contains a clearly defined focus and that there are no other sources of epileptic activity. It is only considered when seizures are frequent enough to severely disrupt the patient's life and cannot be controlled by drugs; and when tests of the patient's intellectual functioning have failed to show evidence of dysfunction in parts of the brain other than the lobe in question. The temporal lobes play an important part in learning and memory. The epileptic activity in the lobe is likely to cause memory impairment so that removal of the lobe will not make this significantly worse provided the opposite temporal lobe is intact. Sometimes there is an improvement in intellectual functioning following temporal lobectomy because there is no longer seizure activity disrupting processing.

Frontal lobectomies and operations to separate the two hemispheres of the brain to prevent the spread of seizure activity from one to the other, are done extremely rarely. This is partly because the kind of epilepsy which would benefit from these operations and which cannot be controlled by drugs is very rare. Such operations can cause behavioural and intellectual changes, and these have to be weighed very carefully against the effect of continuing severe, frequent seizures.

*Behavioural Management*

Sometimes seizure frequency can be reduced by psychological techniques. These may serve to eliminate pseudo-epileptic seizures and to reduce the number of epileptic seizures. The so-called 'psychological' techniques are really a matter of common sense. They can be applied by anyone if done systematically, but it is advisable to consult a psychologist, so that a detailed programme which fits the needs of the individual can be devised. It is important that everyone dealing with the child should follow the same rules, and sometimes a psychologist is the best person to do this by liaising between family and school.

As with all behavioural management programmes the starting point is observation and information gathering. Although there are similarities to the type of information from observation required for making the initial diagnosis, the emphasis is different. As before it is important to note events occurring before the attack and after it, but this time with reference to the situation as a whole.

*Circumstances.*   Place: do seizures occur more often in one particular place than another, e.g. more often at home than at school or vice versa?

Time: do they occur at any particular time of day? Before or after any particular event, e.g. before attending for hospital appointments, or before a school exam?

Other people: note whether any particular person is always present (or absent) at the time of the attack.

State: do they occur when the child is tired, excited, angry, frustrated, hungry or in any other particular physical or emotional state?

*Consequences.*   The course of events following a seizure may raise the child's anxiety about his attacks. This is undesirable in itself and may actually cause an increase in frequency. If, for example, he perceives that other people are panicking, or if he is constantly warned against doing things 'in case you have another fit', he may become quite fearful. If other children ridicule him after the attack or ostentatiously avoid him, this will also raise his anxiety. Obviously, it is impossible entirely to control the behaviour of other children in relation to the child with epilepsy, but to an extent their attitude will reflect that of the adults. The other way in which the consequences of the attack may increase the possibility of further attacks is if they are 'rewarding'. Seizures may serve to gain the attention of a particular person, or to get the child out of an undesirable task. The 'reward' can be very obvious as, for example, when a parent gives the child a special treat to 'make up for' having a seizure; or more subtle, as when the seizures serve to gain the child distinction and importance which he cannot otherwise gain.

Having made these observations and put them together with a description of the course of the seizure, it may be possible to improve management.

*Modification of Circumstances (Place, Time, Other People, State).*   If it is observed that seizures always occur under a particular set of circumstances, then the simplest way to improve management would be to avoid these circumstances. This, however, will often not be practical or desirable. If seizures tend to occur when the child is tired or hungry, then keeping to regular meal times and bed times may help; but if the provocative factors are getting angry or going to school, then obviously simple avoidance is impossible. It may instead be possible to teach him to deal more effectively with stressors so that they cease to trigger attacks. The way in which this can be done will vary according to the age of the child and the particular circumstances. If anxiety is the key factor, then a closer look at what it is about the situation that is producing the anxiety, reassurance and graded exposure may help. A sample case is that of a 9-year-old boy who once had a seizure on his way to school and then got into trouble for being late. It was observed, over the weeks following this, that he had seizures on his way to school more often than at any other time. For a limited period his parents were advised to send him out to school at a time which was early enough to allow him to have a seizure, and still arrive in time. Because of this he ceased to worry about whether or not he had an attack and there was a reduction in frequency. It was then possible to send him to school later and later, until he was back to his normal routine.

Another example of a particular circumstance/state provoking seizures is that of a 4-year-old child who when frustrated or teased became inarticulate with rage, hyperventilated and usually went into a generalised seizure. Management was improved by interrupting this chain of events by picking her up and taking her out of the room as soon as she began hyperventilating. Her parents were encouraged to send her to nursery school so that by mixing with other children her social behaviour would have the opportunity to mature, and she would be better able to tolerate teasing and frustration.

*Modification of Consequences.* There is obviously overlap between 'circumstance' and 'consequence', thus the case of the boy who was anxious about being late for school serves also to illustrate how alteration of the consequence of the seizure — in this case punishment for being late — can improve management.

Eliminating gains and rewards for having a seizure is very effective when these have been observed to be a significant factor. The simple rule is never to pay unnecessary attention to an attack and not let it disrupt the normal routine. Rewarding seizure-free periods can also be effective in the case of a child who is having frequent attacks without any obvious or changeable circumstances and consequences. A star chart with gradually increasing length of time required to achieve a star, or for older children, a monetary reward at the end of seizure-free periods may improve control. Some cases have been quoted of the effective use of punishment for seizures. They were eliminated, for example, in a 10-year-old girl who was given an unpleasant medicine after every seizure.

Often a combination of different techniques will best meet the needs of the individual case, but in general it is better to keep programmes as simple as possible. The proportion of cases likely to respond to behavioural management techniques is entirely unknown, but provided the child and those responsible for him do not have unreasonable expectations of success, it is always worth making the careful observations necessary and making a trial of some change in management. These techniques are not an alternative to drug treatment, but if they improve control in any given case then it may eventually be possible — at the discretion of the child's doctor — to phase out his anti-convulsants.

## Educational Problems

Children with epilepsy are more at risk of having educational and social problems than other children.

*Specific Deficits*

The presence of epilepsy does not necessarily mean that there will be intellectual difficulties, but if the epilepsy is caused by a localised cerebral lesion then the same lesion may also cause a specific intellectual deficit. In normal development the brain becomes more specialised. Different functions — language, memory, reasoning, processing of visual information — become organised from different centres. Any mental activity involves many different areas in different parts of the brain, but it is possible for a lesion at a specific site completely to disrupt one form of activity. The deficit may be obvious, particularly if it is acquired suddenly as a consequence of head injury, but if it is a developmental deficit there is a danger that the child will be considered generally 'slow' and will not receive the specialised teaching that he needs. The kind of teaching will depend on the deficit — whether it is in language skills, memory, attentiveness, etc. — and a detailed discussion of the remediation required is beyond the scope of this text. It is important to emphasise, however, that a child who has epilepsy should not be expected to do less well at school than other children. If he is having difficulty, it is not sufficient to say that it is simply a result of his epilepsy. Every attempt should be made to identify precisely the nature of the difficulty, and it should be remembered that if there is a specific deficit other functions may be average or better.

*Impaired Concentration*

A more common problem than specific intellectual deficit in epileptic children is poor concentration. This may be a direct result of seizures. If a child is building up to, or recovering from a major seizure, concentration may be affected. If he is having frequent absence attacks he will keep missing pieces of information given him. Sometimes his attacks may be 'sub-clinical', that is without observable signs, but may still disrupt his ability to attend. Anti-convulsant medication may also affect concentration by causing sleepiness. There is no easy solution to this problem, but being aware of it may prevent an unduly punitive attitude being adopted by the teachers of an inattentive epileptic child. All children need frequent changes of task if interest and motivation are to be maintained. Epileptic children who have difficulty in concentrating need even more consideration in this respect.

*Absence From School*

School performance can be disturbed by epilepsy if there are frequent absences from school because the child has been kept at home or sent home after a seizure. This may happen because parents are over-protective, or because teachers feel unable to cope with seizures in school. It is always in the child's best interests for him to miss as little school as possible; teachers should be informed about the kind of seizure and what to do if one occurs. This will increase their confidence and will help parents to stop worrying about the consequences of an attack in school.

**Management of Social Problems**

There are many ways in which epilepsy can cause social problems for a child. Some are the result of difficulties he may have in coping with seizures, and some may be the result of the difficulties other people have in coping with his problem and overcoming their prejudices.

*Family*

In some families, where the child's seizures are frequent or severe, there is a tendency for his epilepsy to become the centre of family life. This can occur where parents are unwilling to leave the child on his own or with strangers, and where, as a result of frequent falls and injuries, they have altered their living arrangements to suit him. In extreme cases the child is never left alone, even to go to the lavatory, and he shares a bed with one or other of his parents, who consequently have to sleep in separate rooms. As a result, marital relations become strained, the other children may feel neglected and resentful, and the epileptic child is leading a very abnormal life. Obviously, this situation is undesirable. The first priority is, of course, to bring the child's seizures under better control, but even when this is done both parents and child may find it difficult to give up the previous arrangements because of the interdependency that has built up. It is also possible that the dependency may actually maintain a high seizure frequency and that it is only when this is adjusted that the seizures will come under control. Naturally, there are varying degrees of over-protectiveness, and some precautions against injury during a seizure are necessary, but a child should never be allowed to feel that his epilepsy is the most important part of him.

Some parents find it very difficult to accept a diagnosis of epilepsy in their child. They may feel guilty or angry and may have all kinds of misconceptions. A common one is that epilepsy leads to progressive mental debility or that it is a form of insanity. Such an attitude may lead to defensiveness and the with-holding of important information from the child's doctor or from the school. It may cause them to punish the seizures or to treat the child as though he were mentally handicapped or mentally unbalanced, without proper regard for any real intellectual or emotional problems he may have. Careful re-education can help with both these undesirable extremes, and the grey areas between them. Some doctors prefer not to use the term 'epilepsy' when advising parents about the management of their child. This may be because they are not yet certain of the diagnosis or because they do not want to arouse anxiety and prejudice. If the child does suffer from epilepsy, and it takes time to bring his seizures under control, sooner or later those involved in looking after him will need to have the condition explained to them. This should be done clearly and in such a way as to eliminate unnecessary anxiety, it always being emphasised to the family that they should not expect different standards of behaviour and co-operation from the child with epilepsy than from their other children.

## *Peer Groups*

As the child gets older he may experience great social embarrassment about his seizures: as a result of other children's attitudes or simply because he feels 'different' at the time of his life when he wants to be the same as everyone else. The problem may become even more acute in adolescence. A common difficulty is conflict between not wanting to tell the new boyfriend or girlfriend about the epilepsy, and fear of the consequences of having a seizure when with them. A similar problem can arise with respect to employers. The best solution to these kinds of difficulty is universal education about the nature and forms of epilepsy, thus reducing unnecessary prejudice and discrimination. If everyone knew how to deal with seizures and what to expect, they would become much less alarming and significant for all concerned.

As with any disability, social problems can be minimised by allowing the child to lead as normal a life as possible. This is not to say that genuine difficulties or dangers should be ignored, but that their sphere of influence should be kept to a minimum. With respect to swimming, for example, it is certainly more dangerous for an epileptic child to swim unsupervised than it is for other children. He need not necessarily be banned from swimming altogether, however, if he goes with a competent adult who will know exactly what to do if he has a seizure. The same applies to school trips and any other demanding activity.

The British Epilepsy Association (Crowthorne House, New Wokingham Road, Wokingham, Berks, RG1 3AY) can provide useful booklets and information for families, and also a badge for the child to wear if he wishes. In any case it is useful for anyone prone to epileptic attacks to carry a card giving address, telephone number and details of medicines normally taken, in case of emergency.

If this chapter has a main point, or underlying theme, it is that epilepsy is not an all-or-none phenomenon. There is great variance in its forms and causes and in the associated problems. The message, therefore, is that making the diagnosis is only a small beginning in tackling the problem. The treatment and management are not only the responsibility of the physician, but of all involved — including the patient. It is never enough simply to focus attention on the seizures. The condition should be regarded in the context of its meaning in the child's daily life and its effect on that. In every case the surrounding circumstances will be different and should be looked at independently. Such an approach improves the child's ability to accept and cope with his epilepsy, as well as helping the family to support him in the management of the condition.

## Further Reading

Hopkins, A. (1984) *Epilepsy: The Facts*, London: OUP

Lubar, J.F. and Deering W.M. (1981) *Behavioural Approaches to Neurology*, New York and London: Academic Press
Sutherland, J.M. and Eadie, M.J. (1980) *The Epilepsies: Modern Diagnosis and Treatment*, (3rd edn) Edinburgh and London: Churchill Livingstone

Publications of the British Epilepsy Association will also be found useful, for example:

*Epilepsy: How best to help* (First Aid Guidelines)
*The Schoolchild With Epilepsy: A Guide for Teachers*

# CHAPTER 7

# Spina Bifida

BILL GILLHAM

## The Condition

Between the third and fourth week after conception the neural fold fuses to form the *neural tube*, the basic structure of the central nervous system — the brain and the spinal cord. It is in the partial failure of this process of fusion, at this fundamental stage of development, that the condition known as *spina bifida cystica* has its origins.

This failure of closure results in a greater or lesser failure of development of the spinal cord so that, at birth, spinal tissue may lie exposed on the surface of the back. The extent and location of the spinal lesion will determine the extent of paralysis of the legs, incontinence and so on. But it must be noted that, irrespective of the severity of the lesion, spina bifida may be associated with other developmental defects, e.g. of the heart and bowel.

The accompanying illustration is of a new-born baby with a severe condition (though by no means the most severe), prior to surgery.

### Initial Medical Treatment

Before about 1960 there was little active medical treatment for babies with spina bifida, with the result that over 80 per cent died before reaching school age, most of them within the first few weeks of life. The exposed tissue easily becomes infected and the risk of such conditions as meningitis is high. A combination of improved care of 'at risk' neonates, advances in surgical techniques and improved treatment of infection meant that during the 1960s many more babies with spina bifida survived. By the early 1970s, however, it was apparent that the problems of care created for their parents, and the quality of life for the child, were so appalling that the moral position of a commitment to survival had to be reviewed.

The basic surgical treatment to deal with the opening in the back is relatively straightforward, i.e. removing the redundant membrane covering; making a covering for the spinal cord from other body tissue; then closing the skin defect after some careful undercutting. The baby is normally able to go home within a month, after the surgical wound has healed. But it must not be thought that this is the sum total of the necessary medical treatment for spina bifida. It is, indeed, only the beginning.

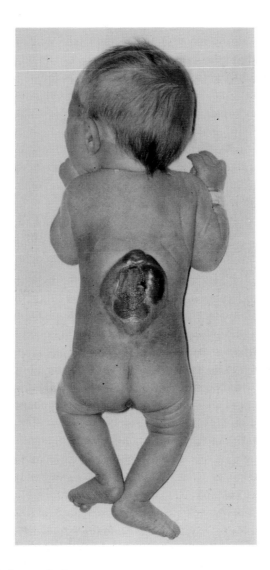

## Treatment of Hydrocephalus

Spina bifida is generally accompanied by hydrocephalus, which is apparent in two-thirds of affected infants even at birth. Because of an associated mal-formation at the base of the brain (the Arnold-Chiari malformation) there is raised intracranial pressure which may show itself in increased head size and enlarged ventricles in the brain with a corresponding risk ot damage.

Because cerebro-spinal fluid, in which the brain and spinal cord are suspended, is almost identical to blood plasma, the condition is usually dealt with by inserting a 'shunt' — a pressure-sensitive, non-return valve — on the side of the head, which draws off into the bloodstream. There are a number of systems, but the basic principle is the same.

The 'shunt' is a remarkably effective piece of medical technology, but complications are nevertheless very common. Apart from the revisions which may be necessary as the child gets older, there are problems of malfunction, as one might expect in a mechanical device, and infection. At a functional level the shunt may become blocked or disconnected. This results in raised intra-cranial pressure with the following possible or probable consequences:

— vomiting
— drowsiness
— headache
— squint
— clumsy gait
— irritability
— loss of concentration
— loss of consciousness

Infection will show itself in symptoms similar to meningitis and can be treated by antibiotics.

For reasons to do both with the basic condition and with the treatment, about a third of children with hydrocephalus have convulsions, which may be frequent and recurrent. The more revisions of the shunt that are necessary the greater the risk of epilepsy developing.

Repeated shunt surgery is one aspect of the quality-of-life problem associated with the condition. However, by school age the production/absorption of cerebro-spinal fluid normally balances out, and the shunt may be removed.

**Treatment and Prognosis: The Moral Dilemma**

Medical practitioners routinely find themselves having to make difficult moral decisions where there is no safe or certain basis for doing so. In the case of the baby with spina bifida it is a responsibility few of us would like to share. Twenty years ago the commitment was generally to saving as many babies as possible: approximately half survived to school age, many having multiple surgery, and with problems of care and pain and mental distress which forced a reconsideration of treatment policy. During the past 10 to 15 years doctors have been more conservative in selecting babies for treatment. At least half of the babies born with spina bifida are not now given treatment: they receive nursing care and are fed orally on demand, but they are not tube fed or given antibiotics. Most of these untreated babies die within the first year of life, but a minority survive, and in a worse state than if they had been treated. Thus, for the medical profession, and for all of us, the moral dilemma has simply shifted. This dilemma has fuelled research into prevention and early detection.

*Causes, Prevalence and Prevention*

The cause of spina bifida and associated neural-tube defects is unknown. Genetic factors probably play a role. In parts of South Wales the incidence is around 1 in 150 births (as compared with 1 in approximately 350 elsewhere in the UK); in parts of North America the incidence is as low as 1 in 1000. We know that the more 'closed' a community is, the more likely it is that genes will come together — because of the restricted gene pool.

It is certainly the case that a woman who has had one spina bifida baby has a much heightened risk of having another — about a 1 in 20 chance, but the associative risk does not follow a straightforward Mendelian pattern, so presumably factors affecting the quality of the intra-uterine environment are also important. The incidence is significantly higher in social classes IV and V as are many other handicapping conditions. Poor diet is probably a contributory factor, and specific foodstuffs have sometimes been proposed as being of particular significance, e.g. substandard potatoes. Dietary improvements reduce the incidence of spina bifida in the babies of 'at risk' women. However, the causal pattern is elusive, and likely to remain so.

An unusual feature of the condition (for which there is no explanation) is that it is more common in females than in males — the reverse of the usual trend. Also females are more likely to be severely affected.

Antenatal diagnosis depends in part on the thoroughness of screening procedures. Routine ultrasound examination will not usually pick up the condition unless an examination of the head and back of the foetus is carried out. Amniocentesis (taking a sample of the amniotic fluid) is not a routine form of screening and can have complications: when employed, however, it can give some indication of the likelihood of the condition.

So while research at this level is clearly important, we cannot at the moment look to prevention or even early diagnosis (assuming that abortion is acceptable) as the answers to the medical and social problems of spina bifida.

## Social, Psychological and Educational Problems of Spina Bifida

There are three questions here:

- what is it like for a family to bring up a child with spina bifida?
- what is it like to be a person with spina bifida?
- what are the distinctive educational needs of the individuals concerned?

*Social and Psychological Problems*

For most children the family, however composed, is the basic social unit: so it is the family which is the main source of care and support for the child with spina bifida.

Bringing up children is, for most parents, the most personally demanding job they take on. The caretaking demands are inherently stressful: the greater the demands, the greater the stress, other things being equal. But for the parents of a spina bifida child the source of stress is not just the enhanced practical demands related to the condition, but also the uncertainties and anxieties that surround it.

Consider the practical and emotional significance of the following problems that go along with the condition:

— commonly, some degree of paralysis of the lower limbs: many children cannot manage without a wheelchair;
— incontinence of urine: a more serious problem for girls than boys since penile urine-collecting devices are relatively effective;
— frequent hospital visits and hospitalisations;
— mortality risk: having made a commitment to the survival of their child, parents have to live with a survival rate not much better than 50/50;
— the possibility of some degree of mental handicap, strongly associated with the extent of hydrocephalus.

The obvious problems of wheelchair management — especially access — can be appreciated. Less obvious is that whoever looks after the child is severely restricted unless they have the use of a car, which may be a financial impossibility, especially if it involves buying a second car.

A special problem with children who have paralysis of the lower limbs and little understanding of self-care is that they may develop pressure sores which they cannot feel, e.g. on the feet and buttocks. If the child is incontinent (and especially if the urine dribbles) chronic sores and ulcers can develop which are very difficult to treat and very distressing to deal with. Bladder control is often a problem in spina bifida, and even when managed efficiently is a constant care-obligation. Like so many of our basic functions which we can take for granted, when it doesn't work properly what has to be done to cope is either tedious, or complicated, or inadequate — or all of those things. And the difficulty is greater as the child gets older. Some children, it is true, become continent, often unpredictably, at around the time of school age. But for most children with a significant degree of paralysis, that cannot be hoped for. For young spina bifida children nappies and manual expression of the bladder are often sufficient: and later on some children can be taught to carry out the latter procedure themselves. But for many children other procedures have to be found, and some of these are complicated, including bypass surgery, although this seems recently to have fallen from favour.

Getting children 'dry' is one of the normal milestones in child-rearing and is always attained with relief; at the same time, a significant proportion of 'normal' children have achieved bladder control only slowly or unreliably — a source of worry to their parents and themselves. Yet these concerns are as nothing compared with the experience of the spina bifida child and his parents. The problem is not simply one of management or of the ulceration and sores that can result from seepage. There is a serious risk of infection and of renal (kidney) failure due to back-pressure from the bladder. It requires an effort of imagination to translate these few details into the daily experience of children and parents in this situation.

At one time it was thought that maternal separation and trauma contingent on hospitalisation permanently damaged the bonding of mother and young child. Such an extreme view is now discredited, but there is no doubt that these separations, especially if recurrent, are both disruptive and distressing. And this is the normal fate of the spina bifida child in a majority of cases. The burden of hospital visits, the confusion for parents and child of seeing a series of medical and paramedical specialists can be imagined. Perhaps less obvious are the effects on other members of the family, especially siblings who have to tolerate this necessary preoccupation with their handicapped brother or sister.

The more conservative treatment policy of recent years has increased the survival rate in the 'treated' group, as one might expect. The explicit choice (and commitment) that parents make under such circumstances, shortly after the child's birth, renders it all the harder to accept that there is still a significant risk that he may not survive to school age. It is not just that the child's death is a shock if it occurs, but that the knowledge of the risk is a constant source of stress while the child is alive.

One of the myths about spina bifida (as, to some extent, is the case with cerebral palsy) is that the child concerned has a normal intelligence trapped in a defective body. It would seem only fair, as some kind of compensation. But the truth, in both cases, is that some degree of retardation is the rule rather than the exception. In respect of spina bifida this is especially true in the case of girls — as previously noted, contrary to the general rule that in handicaps boys come off worst.

The possibility of a degree of mental retardation is particularly hard for many parents to accept, especially as the child may present as 'bright' and chatty. A distinctive characteristic of many children with hydrocephalus — the condition commonly associated with spina bifida — is their tendency to talk fluently and easily — and emptily. This 'cocktail party' syndrome is frequently reported. It is hard to describe — it has to be experienced — but has two features of note:

— it often has little to do with the social context in which it is occurring;
— it is not participatory, i.e. it does not give room for the other person.

Such a conversational flow can be overwhelming and off-putting, although individuals' reactions to continuous chatter vary, as one might expect. It is certainly difficult to accept that a child so fluent in speech can be poor in thought and reasoning: but such is often the case.

And what of the child behind all this? In part the forced social chatter is probably linked to the child's attempt to make up for the social experiences he or she has missed, is always missing. Being social depends very much on the ability to move around, to approach other people and interact with them. Intellectual development too depends on the ability to explore, to handle things, to check out expectations, to experiment. Personal effectiveness, both social and intellectual, depends upon the ability to take action; and in many ways this is denied to the wheelchair child.

This dependent state and his (necessary) expectation that he can call on other people for help means that the child may be less *socialised* (although 'sociable') when he comes of school age. And, in turn, this affects his ability to relate to peers who will be less understanding and responsive.

The fuller implications of his condition come only with adolescence, when the gap between him and his peers becomes evident in relation to future careers, sexual opportunities, and the extravagant ambitions normal in the young, the fit and the untried. It is here that the mental pain is the greatest, and for those who see themselves as responsible the moral question the most difficult.

*Educational Problems*

As previously mentioned, it is a common assumption that spina bifida children are normal intellectually and have normal upper limb function. However, although some are of superior intelligence, most are below average, and a sizeable minority are mentally handicapped. Impairment of upper limb function is not always readily apparent, but is more common than might be supposed.

Along with the assumption of normal intelligence has been the expectation that children with spina bifida should attend normal school; whilst this is often both desirable and feasible, ordinary schools vary enormously in their willingness to accept a handicapped child and meet his particular needs. But for all schools there are three overriding factors affecting their ability to cater for the spina bifida child: educational level, degree of mobility, and management of toileting, especially if he is incontinent. Special schools are required when the management of the handicap is difficult and/or educational progress is very slow; or when no suitable ordinary school is available convenient to where the child lives. There are no hard-and-fast rules about placement: decisions have to be made in individual circumstances, bearing in mind the needs of the child and what can, conceivably, be provided.

For the wheelchair child to function efficiently in a normal school a classroom assistant is likely to be essential. Adaptation to steps and toilets is an obvious necessity, but access and movement generally have to be considered carefully. However, facilities alone are not enough. An ordinary school's ability to accept a handicapped child depends largely on the attitudes of the staff *as a whole,* but to a significant extent on outside interest and support that may be lacking. Placements can break down because the school finds itself struggling without the benefit of practical help and advice; or of interest and appreciation.

Individual teachers vary in their ability to cope with a range of attainments in the children in their teaching group. The spina bifida child who is an efficient learner has a good chance of keeping his place, whatever mobility problems there may be, because he is, in fact, less demanding than the 'normal' slow learner. But they are often slow learners themselves and not uncommonly display specific learning disabilities, e.g. perceptual confusions which affect not only writing but the use of such simple and precise 'tools' as scissors. These difficulties may not be apparent at all until school age and may only gradually be recognised there. Fine hand control is basic to much of school work, and quite a small impairment can cause considerable difficulties. For example, the spina bifida child may have difficulty in keeping the book or paper still when trying to write, so that the result is often very poor. The illustration shows a piece of apparatus (rather like a draughtsman's drawing board) which will grip the book or paper at the top, so maximising the child's performance.

This kind of equipment is typical of the 'adapted environment' approach to design which is fundamental to minimising the handicap caused by disability. Even something as simple as a modified pencil grip can greatly improve performance — and therefore motivation because of the child's increased satisfaction in what he has achieved.

It is not suggested that all difficulties are so easily overcome. Children with spina bifida, like those with cerebral palsy, often have visual perceptual difficulties which affect their ability to read; somewhat similar to the difficulties manifested by children who are sometimes called 'dyslexic'.

Taking part in sporting activities, even for those who need a wheelchair, will also improve hand/eye co-ordination and control — quite apart from the enjoyment gained from increasing skill, or the opportunities for mixing socially with others less handicapped.

## Future Prospects

Fewer severely handicapped children are being allowed to survive, so the prospects for the majority of those who do are correspondingly better. But the decision process is an uneasy one, and no-one can be satisfied with it. Improvements in wheelchair facilities and the opportunities for the disabled to enter more fully into society are likely to continue: to the benefit of the present generation of spina bifida children.

Refinements in medical technology depend upon research funding and priorities, and these are currently under pressure so that the rate of progress there is likely to slow down. Early, i.e. prenatal detection is perhaps particularly important because it is at this stage that the difficult decisions are most easily made; but reliable detection, especially at the level of general screening, is still in the future. Prevention is another matter because of the unpredictability of the handicap (except in families with other affected members).

Some parts of this chapter make gloomy reading: they are the parts of the story we would like to forget. Some children have a mild condition, without significant handicap, or are wheelchair-bound but very able: many others are not so fortunate. The most difficult problem in spina bifida — as in some others, such as cerebral palsy and muscular dystrophy — is helping the child to adjust to the implications of his disability. And it is a problem precisely because it is difficult for the rest of us to face up to.

## Further Reading

Anderson, E.M. and Spain, B. (1977) *The Child with Spina Bifida*, London: Methuen
Russell, P. (1984) *The Wheelchair Child* (2nd edn), London: Souvenir Press
Stark, G.D. (1977) *Spina Bifida: Problems and Management*, Oxford: Blackwell

The Association for Spina Bifida and Hydrocephalus
Tavistock House North
Tavistock Square
London WC1 9HJ
Tel: 01 388 1382
promotes the interests of this group and disseminates information.

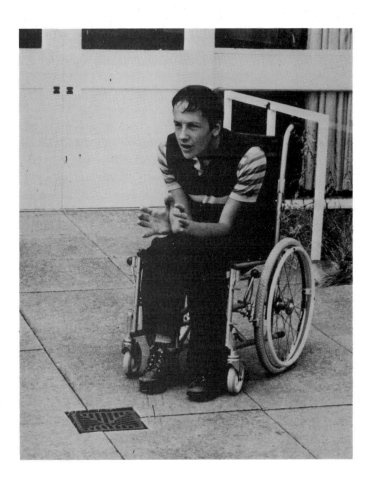

# CHAPTER 8

# Autism

DEREK WILSON

## Profiles of Autism

*George* is 8 years old and attends a school for children with severe learning difficulties. He has no spoken language and is being taught to sign using his hands. In five months George has been able to learn 12 signs which he will use to request a drink, various foodstuffs, music to be played, etc. As his repertoire of signs expands it becomes more difficult to teach him new signs. George has great difficulty in learning all new skills, and continues to require help and supervision with toileting, feeding and dressing. He is typically a very passive child, who seems content to spend long periods of time sitting or lying on the floor searching for pieces of thread or hairs which he will wind and unwind round his fingers. George enjoys music and can occasionally be heard humming a recognisable tune to himself. He also likes to travel by car or bus, and his parents have noticed how observant he is on outings, noting all deviations from familiar routes to the point of being aware that at traffic lights they are queue-ing in a different lane from the one they normally take. His parents know George is aware of these changes because he is upset by them and his behaviour can become difficult to manage. He will typically bite his hand and scream when upset, but as he has become older this behaviour has lessened. The main problem experienced by George's parents and teachers at present lies in finding activities that will sustain his interest during teaching. As his mother says: 'George's best skill is remaining unchanged despite all the things we try and do to get him interested and get him to learn'.

*Claire* is 4 years old and is an extremely active child who seems to require little sleep and is frequently awake for 18-19 hours daily. Claire walked at 9 months and since then has required constant supervision. She has no apprecia-tion of common dangers and her parents need to restrain her on outings. She will often walk on tiptoe and is an agile climber, but is unable to pedal a tri-cycle. Claire is not toilet-trained and screams if sat on a potty or toilet. Her parents felt her language was normal up to the age of 18 months, when she fell and gashed her leg and this required stitching. In the weeks following the acci-dent Claire used her language less and less, and by her second birthday she was not talking at all. She did not speak again until she was $2^{1}/_{2}$, when she saw a toilet on television and said 'flush the water'. At age 4 she is able to speak in sentences. Her parents find it difficult to hold a conversation with her, however, and she will often reply to questions by repeating the question itself.

At other times she will ignore her parents, and they find it difficult to get Claire to look at them or at an object they want her to take an interest in. Claire completely ignores other children, and although she attends a local playgroup most of her time there is spent collecting whatever material or clothing she can find and draping it over chairs. She is especially fond of velvety material. Claire can be clingy with her parents in new situations or when strangers are present, but would have no hesitation in approaching and touching a stranger if he or she were wearing velvet. Claire's behaviour has become a little less volatile as she has grown older, although she will scream violently when thwarted or diverted from her favourite pursuits. Her parents feel that her main problem is in learning to communicate and to use the ability to learn, which they feel she has. They do not think that Claire is 'mentally handicapped', but cannot imagine a school that would be able to teach her.

George and Claire differ widely in their overall levels of attainment, ability to communicate, and in the management problems they pose for their parents; yet both children share the same diagnosis of their difficulties — autism. They have been described in some detail to show something of the range of behaviours and developmental problems that can stem from the underlying impairments that both children have in common. Before looking in detail at the nature and description of these underlying impairments, it is necessary to point out that a variety of different labels are and have been used to describe the children discussed in this chapter. The basic terms 'autism' and 'autistic' will be used here, but readers who undertake further reading will come across a diversity of terms, and it will often be unclear whether a similar or different group of children is intended from those discussed here. A brief glossary of terms is therefore included at the end of this chapter.

## Definition and Diagnosis

The diversity of terms in use reflects the fact that of all the diagnostic and descriptive labels applied to children, the term 'autism' continues to be one of the most controversial and misunderstood. There are many reasons for this, but the simplest is that there are no precise clinical tests or objective physical signs that can be used to confirm in every case that a child is or is not autistic. People unfamiliar with autistic children are often struck initially by their outward appearance of normality, and in fact a diagnosis of autism can be made only by taking a detailed history of the child's development and by closely observing the child's behaviour. This fact sets autism apart from the majority of conditions described in this book.

Most people with experience of autistic children feel confident in identifying the condition despite the lack of 'objective' signs. With an intimate knowledge of such children over a period of time, one becomes aware of the striking similarities that can exist between individual children despite wide differences in age, social class, family background and other factors which have an import-ant influence on children's development. Often these similarities will be evident in the actual detail of their conversation and in the specific content of their interests. However, as will be clear from the profiles of George and Claire, overall levels of attainment and the extent of the actual learning difficulty experienced by autistic children can vary widely, making it impossible to give a *single* description of a typical autistic child.

## History and Early Development

The use of the term 'autistic' has its beginnings in the work of the American child psychiatrist Leo Kanner, who in 1943 published an account of the prob-lems of eleven children seen by him over a number of years. Kanner was impressed by the similarities between these children, and felt that he had evid-ence of a hitherto unrecognised syndrome which he termed 'early infantile autism'. The eleven children seemed to have several abnormalities in common. They seemed to make very little ordinary social contact with other people and at times would actively avoid doing so, preferring to remain aloof and in a world of their own. They seemed upset by changes in their surroundings and would often act to 'preserve sameness' (e.g. in the positions of familiar objects). Generally, such children seemed fascinated by objects (as opposed to people), and would show skill in their handling and manipulation of objects. Some of the children did not use language, and those that did speak did so unusually and without an ability to make normal conversation. Finally, Kanner was struck by the fact that many of the children seemed to have an intelligent and alert facial expression, and he felt that, despite their abnormal behaviours, they were of good cognitive potential. Evidence of these five areas of abnorm-ality in a child constituted the syndrome of early infantile autism. A 'syndrome' in this context means a characteristic group of patterns of behaviours shown by the child, and the fact that autism is viewed as a syndrome has very important implications for much of what follows. Crucial to the notion of a syndrome is the important point that no single behaviour by itself provides sufficient evidence of the condition, and for a diagnosis to be made we need to observe *several* characteristic behaviours.

The developmental history of the behaviours is also an important factor in diagnosis, and there is general agreement today that there should be evidence of the onset of the difficulties before the age of 30 months. In the majority of cases there will be evidence of difficulties from infancy, but there will be some children who are autistic for whom it is difficult to find evidence of problems in the early months of their lives.

Early interpretations of Kanner's first description of the syndrome by other clinicians tended to look to the five areas of difficulty already discussed, and include onset before 30 months, as the criteria for diagnosis. As others began to carry out their own diagnostic work, however, it became clear that there was a need to make these criteria more objective and more easily applied to individual children. In the 40 years since Kanner's original study there have been several attempts to do this. In 1961 Mildred Creak produced an aid to diagnosis that listed 9 points, or areas, of abnormality that can be observed in autistic children; and again, in 1971 another psychiatrist, Rendle-Short, produced a 14-point formulation. Such attempts to make diagnosis more objective adopt the approach of listing unusual and typical autistic behaviours in detail, but are limited by the fact that no one autistic child is likely to show all the behaviours listed. Therefore, a numerical criterion was required to decide whether the diagnosis is appropriate in a particular case: for example, if a child can be observed to be displaying more than half the behaviours from a list of 14, then he should be seen as autistic; less than half, then the diagnosis is in doubt. However, further confusions are produced by doing this. By accepting, say, 7 from 14 behaviours on a list as being sufficient, it would be quite possible to diagnose a child as autistic who shows no difficulty in forming social relationships and therefore quite unlike any of the children described by Kanner.

Clearly, there was a need to group the difficulties seen in autistic children into some sort of hierarchy, and list those behaviours which are basic to the syndrome (primary manifestations) and invariably present separately from those behaviours which are a consequence of the primary difficulties (secondary manifestations) and not invariably present. This has been the approach adopted by later workers in the UK — notably Michael Rutter, Lorna Wing and Elizabeth Newson — who have each made important contributions to the general agreement that exists today over the diagnostic criteria for autism. Elizabeth Newson's formulation is discussed in detail in the following section.

## The Primary Difficulties of Autistic Children

1. Impairment of language and all modes of communication, including gesture, facial expression and other 'body language' and the timing of these.
2. Impairment of social relationships, in particular a failure of social empathy.
3. Evidence of rigidity and inflexibility of thought processes.
4. Onset before 30 months.

All four criteria need to be met. The first three describe the basic impairments that underlie the condition, and evidence of their existence is found by observation of the child and by detailed discussion with his parents on the development of the child, and particularly the development of social awareness in infancy.

The actual behaviours that are evidence of each of the basic impairments are, of course, many and varied, and there are degrees of severity. Over one-half of all autistic children show severe learning difficulties, and a small percentage will function on an average or above-average level. Thus, subsequent research has shown that Kanner's early impression that autistic children had good cognitive potential was found to be true of only a small minority.

The initial impressions made by autistic children will vary widely as is evident in the profiles of George and Claire. This can make diagnosis difficult, and it is important that the nature of the basic impairments is clearly understood before actual behaviour can be correctly interpreted. Some typical behaviours and difficulties that stem from the underlying impairment are discussed below.

### Impairment of Communication

No autistic child has normal language (verbal or non-verbal). For some children speech itself will never be acquired; others will develop and use single words but no rules of syntax for combining these into phrases and sentences. Others will develop speech in sentences with appropriate syntax, but the pragmatics, rules for use of language in real situations of communication, will not be acquired. Where speech is acquired it will often be characterised by *echolalia*: a tendency to reply to questions and requests by repetition of what the child has just heard, i.e. the question or the request itself. Echolalic speech is often recognisable as such because it tends to be at a better syntactical level and have a more expressive intonational quality than the child's non-echolalic, spontaneous utterances. Echolalia need not involve immediate repetition of what the child has heard, and some echolalic phrases become part of the child's repertoire for dealing with a variety of questions and requests (*delayed echolalia*).

Comprehension of spoken language and non-verbal expression (e.g. body posture, facial expression, miming) also pose problems for autistic children. Difficulties can range from the understanding of only a few single words to failure to grasp the more subtle nuances of what is said, e.g. where the literal content of what is said is qualified by facial expression — raised eyebrows, tongue in cheek, etc. All autistic children make very limited use of gesture in their communication, and where there is some development of non-verbal expressiveness (usually not until late childhood/adolescence), difficulty is often apparent in the timing and synchronising of this, such that it will seldom give the impression of matching or flowing with the spoken content of a conversation. Impairment of communication will usually be evident in autistic children from infancy, and parents will often recall difficulty in communicating with their child at the preverbal level of lap games, singing games, surprise games and in setting up and sustaining a 'conversation without words'. Some autistic children will appear to have had a period where their language was felt by parents to have been developing normally and then appear to 'lose' their communication skills, sometimes temporarily, sometimes permanently. This abnormal pattern of development is poorly understood. In some cases detailed questioning of parents will reveal that the period of 'normal development' was in fact quite unlike a normal child's acquisition of language in that the child seemed to be 'collecting' words (usually nouns) without any real ability to use them for communication with others. If the child subsequently does not use these words, what is lost is not the ability to communicate but simply the child's interest in expanding or maintaining his 'collection'.

## Impairment of Social Relationships

The autistic child's difficulty here lies in his limited awareness of the intentions and feelings of other people, and does not necessarily involve a lack of attachment or affection towards familiar adults or children (although where attachment is evident it will seldom be expressed in the same way as an ordinary child's). In fact, many older autistic children are clearly happiest and most secure in the presence of those adults they know best. Some professionals are confused by this, believing that unless a child is aloof and indifferent to other people he cannot be described as autistic. Many autistic children do, however, pass through a stage of seeming aloofness or indifference, and this is typically most evident in early childhood before the age of 5. Some will continue throughout childhood to actively avoid close physical contact, e.g. cuddling, and seem to find it very unrewarding. The same children, however, will often be found positively to enjoy rough-and-tumble play with adults (although seldom with other children) and meaningful eye-to-eye contact, and laughter that has a natural and 'giggly' feel to it will often come easily to children who are played with in this fashion. It is more typical, however, for patterns of eye contact to be abnormal and unusual.

The picture here is a complex one, and it is not simply the case that autistic children do not make or avoid making eye contact with other people. The eye movements and direction of gaze of ordinary children can give us very accurate information as to what a child is experiencing and is aware of. Autistic children's eye movements, when interacting with other people, typically suggest a profound lack of awareness of the reactions of others. This will be very evident during attempts at conversation and while engaged in a mutual task as in a teaching situation. Very little visual attention may be paid to another's face at such times, and autistic children are generally able to make very little use of other people's facial expressions for information and confirmation. A normal child's visual attention will come and go from an adult's face during a conversation or activity, and it will be especially responsive to changes in the adult's voice tone or volume, or at certain key stages in a task, e.g. on completion. None of this would typically be evident in an autistic child. He may pay very little attention to others' faces or he may tend to look 'too much' and stare. What will be lacking will be the feeling that he is keeping in touch with the state of mind and the intentions of the other person and making reference to them by eye contact. The autistic child may not realise that there is information to be had by making eye contact, or at a later stage he may realise that changes are taking place in another person's face but be unclear as to what these changes mean. It is important to be clear about the whole question of eye contact in autistic children as it is often mistakenly said that a child who makes eye contact is unlikely to be autistic. In fact, it is the timing and the quality of the eye contact that is made and the social awareness suggested by this rather than the sheer quantity of eye contact that is important.

If the difficulties that give rise to unusual eye contact are clearly understood, then the nature of the impairment of social awareness underlying autism will be evident. 'Aloof' is an inaccurate description of autistic children's social behaviour because it implies that the child so described has made some sort of decision *not* to interact with or relate to other people, and that there is an element of deliberate rejection of interaction involved. Use of the adjective 'aloof' tells us more about our feelings as adults when we are unable to gain and sustain an autistic child's attention and interest. The reality is that the autistic child's difficulties in achieving social awareness are profound, and he is not so much 'aloof' from us as unable to make sense of us.

### Evidence of Rigidity in Cognitive Development

This is the most difficult area of impairment to give a clear account of; yet it is vital to the diagnosis and education of autistic children that we have insight into the difficulties experienced by the children at every developmental stage in forming concepts and expanding their intellectual understanding of the world. An understanding of these difficulties will also help to make clearer how autistic children functioning at a very low developmental level differ from the general population of children with severe learning difficulties, and likewise how able autistic children who can participate in an ordinary school curriculum differ from normal children of the same age.

It is helpful to look at symbolic and pretend play with objects to try to understand the nature of these difficulties more clearly.

In many autistic children it will be impossible to find any clear evidence of pretend play at any stage of their development, and the usual toys that are made available for all children by their parents will tend to be 'played with' in a quite different fashion by autistic children. Toy cars may simply be played with by arranging them in straight lines or by turning them upside down and spinning their wheels. This activity does not represent either 'traffic jams' or 'repairs to tyres', but are simply the only uses of toy cars that are perceived. The crucial step in normal cognitive development that allows children to perceive that one object can be used to stand for another is invariably problematic for autistic children. In this example it may be that they have two quite separate concepts of a 'car': one for the large noisy object that you travel in, and another for the small objects that you can hold in your hand and make patterns on the floor with. Autistic children find difficulty in applying the first concept to the second to generate pretend play, and this is one example of what is meant when it is said that these children show rigidity in cognitive development. A proportion of autistic children will, however, develop some ability to pretend in their play and may learn to put dolls to bed and give them drinks, etc. This is unusual, and will tend to be seen only in the more able child where such 'pretending' has been *deliberately taught* and encouraged by parents or teachers. However, even pretend play of this sort will show evidence of rigidity in as much as it is typically carried out in a highly stereotyped and repetitive fashion. It does not get elaborated in a creative way, but tends to become a routine type of activity which is simply repeated by the child without significant variation in content. This is an example of a general problem met by those responsible for the education of autistic children, namely a failure to effectively generalise what has been learnt in one situation and apply it to fresh situations.

These difficulties are experienced by autistic children in all areas of their cognitive development and do not simply limit the quality of their symbolic play. As is often the case when we attempt to understand autistic children, the essence of the problem can most clearly be seen when the difficulties encountered by the more able and verbal children are looked at. The following episode demonstrates a rigid formation of the concepts of 'animate' and 'inanimate' in an 8-year-old autistic boy, and shows the extreme vulnerability of his understanding of the world.

On an initial visit to a special school, Ian, an 8-year-old relatively able boy, encounters David, a younger boy who has no spoken language. Ian has never met a child with no speech before and is clearly puzzled and confused by someone who cannot talk. Ian asks many questions about David: 'When will he talk? Does he not want to talk? Is he a baby?' School staff seem to have little success in putting Ian's mind at rest, and Ian eventually asks if David is 'dead'. Staff reassure Ian that this is not the case. Ian is then silent for a time but his behaviour becomes increasingly restless and agitated. A short while later he is seen standing near a rocking horse even more agitated, and asking staff if the horse is 'going to talk'.

This episode demonstrates the need for those involved with autistic children to have a very clear understanding of the nature of their difficulties, because it would be all too easy to perceive Ian's behaviour in this situation as simply incomprehensible or bizarre and his questions as quite mad. What has happened is that Ian has been unable to integrate 'David' with his own current understanding of what things are dead and what things are alive. Prior to encountering David, Ian's understanding is approximately: if a thing can talk it is alive; if not, it is dead — unless it is a baby, hence Ian's third question. Now he has come across an exception to this rule, for David cannot talk but also he is not dead. As an autistic child Ian cannot come to terms with this discrepancy so becomes anxious. Even more seriously, his existing concepts and understanding seem shaken by the discovery of 'David', and he is for a time quite unsure what to expect of objects that now may be animate. Hence, he seeks reassurance that the rocking horse will not begin to talk.

Note here that it is not abnormal to be puzzled by a child who cannot talk, and most ordinary children would be interested and confused by this. What is abnormal is the difficulty Ian has in dealing with the new information and in expanding his ideas to allow for such a possibility. Also, it is worth stressing the crucial importance of the particular area of cognitive development that is threatened by this episode. Clear ideas about what is alive and what is not are vital to our entire understanding of the world and to our ability to predict what will happen, and without them the world would quickly become a very frightening place. This type of confusion over the animation or otherwise of objects is not uncommon in autistic children who are able to form concepts at this level, and can be long lasting. The likelihood in Ian's case is that his concepts will not develop sufficiently to accept the idea of 'David', and that the adults around Ian will be repeatedly questioned over a long period about the encounter as he attempts to resolve the contradiction and maintain the integrity of his concepts.

An understanding of these cognitive difficulties helps to make sense of much of the ritualistic and compulsive behaviour typical of autistic children, and gives further meaning to Kanner's original observation of a 'need to preserve sameness'. Autistic children have only a limited grasp of the world and of its constantly shifting experiences. Little wonder then that they strive to maintain things as they know them and object to changes in their world; that they impose their own rituals and routines on it to enable them to control and predict with greater certainty.

In describing the basic impairments underlying autism under three separate headings, there is a danger of creating the impression that it is possible to understand the effects of these impairments in isolation from each other. This is not the case, and a worthwhile understanding of autism can be achieved only when it is remembered that autistic children function like the rest of us, as whole beings and not as individuals with three types of problem. It does not make sense to attempt to apportion the cause of any particular failure or learning difficulty seen in autistic children to any one of the basic impairments. Each is inextricably tied in with the others, and all mutually influence the overall development of the child. This is what is meant when we call a child 'autistic' — each of the basic impairments acting together to produce a unique set of developmental problems.

As a brief example of what is meant, it is helpful to consider the problems that all autistic children have with humour. Even the most able autistic individuals are typically quite unable to create humour by joke-telling, or to share in humour generated by another person. A full analysis is not possible here, but even a brief consideration of what is involved in being humorous will point out that each of the areas of human skill that are impaired in autism is required.

For example, the telling of even the simplest joke or funny story requires the teller to be able to command and time his spoken language in step with the reactions he perceives in his audience; it requires a clear understanding of what expectations he will have set up before delivering the punchline; the ability to recognise a 'joke' for what it very often is — a play on concepts and on the idiomatic uses of language or on the fact that words can sound the same and have different meanings (e.g. 'what is black and white and red (read) all over?') and so on. It is no surprise that autistic children are sometimes described as very 'serious' children, because given the basic impairments they suffer from, they are impossibly placed when it comes to producing or participating in conventional children's humour. It is also clear from this example that it is fruitless to try to say which of the impairments contributes most (or least) to their problems with humour.

## The Search for Causes: Indications and Evidence

Autism is a rare condition; prevalence figures from several sources are in good agreement in reporting a rate of 4-5 cases of autism per 10,000 children. This fact has a number of implications. First, the overall numbers of children that are typically available for study by research workers are invariably small, and this continually limits the reliability of any conclusions that might be drawn. Secondly, the rarity of autism severely restricts opportunities that the vast majority of all professional workers will have to develop a first-hand knowledge of the condition for more than one or two cases; and as we have already seen there are clear dangers in generalising from one autistic child to another. This point is discussed further when the educational needs of autistic children are considered.

Sex differences in the incidence of autism are clearly evident when a large group of autistic children is studied and autistic boys outnumber girls by a ratio of 4:1. The sex difference is most obvious when the group of children looked at is restricted to those cases where the diagnosis is very clear cut (see glossary — *nuclear autism*). Although more boys than girls are affected there is a tendency for girls to be more seriously handicapped by the condition than are boys, and the preponderance of boys over girls is less striking when the analysis is restricted to those most severely affected.

We have already seen that the vast majority of autistic children will show overall delay in the development of their attainments when compared with ordinary children, and that there are degrees in the severity of the delay. This fact has led researchers to look for the cause of autism in some kind of brain damage or malfunction. However, there is seldom any evidence of obvious neurological abnormalities in young autistic children on examination, and the main reason for believing that organic neurological difficulties underlie autism is that as many as 30 per cent of autistic children will have had epileptic fits by the time they are young adults. This fact suggests that there is an actual physical abnormality of brain function that later leads to the development of epilepsy or epileptic episodes. This connection is no more than suggestive, however, because it is also clear that the majority of autistic children will continue to show no neurological abnormality into adolescence and adulthood.

Also, it may be the case, as will be discussed in more detail later, that the autism itself produces the evidence of abnormal brain function (epilepsy) and not vice versa.

The depressing reality is that the cause or causes of autism are unknown and look likely to remain so for the foreseeable future. What is now clear is the general direction in which answers are likely to be found, and that it is unlikely that one single common cause that is shared by all affected children will be uncovered by research. Thus, there is now general agreement that autism is produced by an organic impairment of some sort and does not arise as a result of psychological (e.g. emotional disturbance) or social factors. This belief has not always been held, however, and early workers felt that the cause of autistic behaviour should be sought in the parents and, in particular, in unusual and damaging child-rearing practices. Today it is only necessary to mention this type of theory in order to refute it. There is, in fact, no evidence of any sort that the parents of autistic children differ significantly from any other group of parents in how they bring up their children. This is not to say that parents of autistic children will always be able to handle their child just as they would an ordinary child. Indeed, this is seldom likely to be the case given what we already know of the children's difficulties and in particular their obsessive and ritualistic behaviour. Moreover, studies of children who have grown up in conditions of extreme deprivation do not present with difficulties that are anything like those of autistic children. Kanner himself felt that there was an observable 'personality type' amongst the parents of autistic children and believed that a predisposition towards becoming autistic may have been inherited by autistic children from their parents. Extensive research has again failed to find clear evidence of this.

Although it is believed that autism is the result of organic abnormality, there are few clues available as to its precise nature, or indeed whether only one type of abnormality should be sought. There may be several possible causes of the syndrome. This seems likely because wherever researchers have looked for a single common cause in the prenatal, perinatal and postnatal histories of children later diagnosed as autistic, no clear pattern has emerged that is shared by all children. Some will have histories of birth difficulty or post-natal infection, others will have histories of prenatal complications (e.g. maternal illness). Overall, when a group of autistic children are looked at for evidence of the range of factors which place children 'at risk' of showing developmental problems, a higher incidence of such factors will be found compared with children developing normally. The difficulty is that not all children with such histories develop autism, while many autistic children will be found whose histories do not show any evidence of such potentially damaging episodes.

Other approaches to the problem of what causes autism have investigated whether links can be found between brain function and body chemistry. A great number of variables have been looked at here, and any detailed examination of research is well beyond the scope of this book and the expertise of this author. It is worth noting, however, that considerable caution is needed when interpreting any findings which appear to show 'pathological' variations in peripheral body-fluid composition in autistic children, and then suggest that these variations are related to the cause of autism. The overriding difficulty for researchers in this area is the fact that so little is known about the biochemical basis of normal behaviour, and therefore it is seldom possible to generate a testable hypothesis which might begin to help us understand autistic behaviour. Furthermore, autistic children behave oddly in any case, e.g. they may engage in long periods of self-stimulatory behaviour such as rocking or running to and fro. We do not have any idea what effects such unusual activity patterns might have on body chemistry, so any reasonable differences that are found might be the result of the odd behaviour itself rather than be related to the cause or underlying biochemical impairment.

It is unlikely that there will be any sudden advances in our knowledge of the biochemical factors which underlie autism: answers to existing puzzles will be highly complex and will be based on other developments in our understanding of the biochemistry of normal behaviour and its developmental process.


**Educational Issues**

Autistic children are educated in almost every type of school — ordinary and special — but because the majority of the children affected by the syndrome will show marked delay in overall development, most will be found in special schools and units of one type or another. A significant number receive education, often on a residential basis, in schools that have been established specifically to meet the needs of autistic children. Many of these schools have been set up by the National Autistic Society (the UK national charity for autistic children and adults). These schools are independent in the sense that they are managed by charitable organisations and not by local education authorities, and depend for their income on the willingness of LEAs to sponsor the attendance of children by payment of fees to the charity. The National Autistic Society will never be in a position to meet the need for school places of all affected children in this country from its own resources, but in the past 15 years the Society has made an outstanding contribution to our understanding of how best to educate and provide for autistic children.

Local education authorities have a statutory duty to ensure that the special educational needs of all children with learning difficulties are met, and also maintain a number of schools and units for autistic children throughout the country. Despite the existence of both independent and local authority provision, finding a suitable school placement for many autistic children poses problems because the demand for places within specialised schools and units will typically be greater than the number of available places. This inevitably leads to placement of autistic children within schools (e.g. schools for children with severe learning difficulties) that do not always have the resources to meet the children's needs.

## Special Educational Provision for Autistic Children

The majority of autistic children will generally be found to make best progress in overcoming their difficulties where a school is able to provide an educational regime as follows:

*1. A Highly Favourable Staff-child Ratio.* One adult to three children is a generally accepted minimum and allows for teaching to be provided within the school day on an individual basis, and for this teaching to be planned on the basis of unique individual learning programmes.

*2. A Curriculum Which Emphasises the Development of Communication Skills.* This will emphasise the teaching of both verbal and non-verbal communication, e.g. sign language, and will use speech-therapy support in the planning and practice of this.

*3. A Regime Able to Tolerate and Contain Disruptive and Disturbing Behaviour.* High levels of staff supervision of children's activity are required, and emphasis will be placed on the training of basic self-help and living skills. Clinical/educational psychology support in the planning and practice of this is typically required.

*4. Contact and Consultation with Parents.* Parents need to be involved closely in all of the above, and consulted on the best educational and social programmes for their child.

In practice this type of educational regime has been most commonly available within special schools for autistic children. However, concern continues to be expressed within special education in general about the practice of setting up such 'segregated' schools and units. There is a body of opinion which feels that the segregated approach is unnecessary and can be disadvantageous to the children themselves.

## Problems of Segregation

The main drawback perceived in segregated education is the absence of appropriate models of ordinary social behaviour for individual autistic children. The peer-group in a school for the autistic will consist solely of other autistic children whose social behaviour will typically be deviant, unlikely to encourage more normal patterns of interaction and, it is argued, may actually worsen the individual child's behaviour. This argument has some force, and a policy of educating autistic children together can produce situations where several children may be showing severely disruptive and acting out behaviour which is intimidating to other more passive autistic children, and serves to heighten their withdrawal from interaction. This is a real danger, and underlines the need for high levels of staff supervision to ensure that the effects of other children's disturbed behaviour on less disruptive children are minimised. As to the absence of appropriate models of social behaviour in schools for autistic children, there is little evidence that such children are able to benefit from simply being exposed to other children interacting in an ordinary fashion; and if this were the case then it is doubtful whether they should properly be described as autistic. In the event, whatever these children learn about appropriate ways of behaving in social situations tends to be achieved as a result of the *direct* teaching of behaviour by adults.

In practice, segregated schools for autistic children have proved manageable, and produce educational advantages which outweigh any negative peer-group effects. One major advantage is that segregated schools will tend to foster the development of staff expertise with autistic children. The individual teacher within a segregated school is clearly in a much better position to reach a full understanding of the real nature and extent of autistic children's difficulties than his or her counterpart in a generic school who may only have experience of a single child. This is important because, as we have seen, autism is a complex and confusing condition, and the children themselves are particularly at risk of being misunderstood by adults or of not having the extent of their difficulties properly appreciated and catered for in the actual teaching input that is offered.

It is likely, therefore, that segregated education, both independent and state maintained, will continue to be seen as the best provision for the majority of autistic children. It is also likely to become increasingly specialised — as our understanding of what forms of educational input are most effective develops — and last for an increasingly long period, as new living situations and continuing education become available for autistic children into early adulthood and beyond.

## Glossary of Diagnostic Labels

*Autistic features*: Some children with developmental difficulties are described as having 'autistic features' rather than as 'autistic'. This may mean several things:

(i) The child may have difficulties associated with another type of handicap, e.g. visual problems, Down's syndrome, and it is felt that the autistic behaviours shown by the child are best understood as being secondary to the other difficulty.

(ii) The child may not show clear evidence of each of the three main areas of basic impairment and therefore the diagnosis is in doubt. A study of children in one London borough found that the incidence figure of children who had autistic features of this sort was as high as 15 in every 10,000 children.

(iii) The child *is* properly described as autistic but his difficulties have not been fully recognised or labelled. Use of the term 'autistic features' in this context may be a consequence of professionals' uncertainty, or because there is a local absence of appropriate educational provision for the child.

*Childhood schizophrenia* is a label only likely to be used to describe autistic children in publications in the 1950s and 1960s. It is not now in general use in the UK as an alternative term for autism, and its use is confined to describe the difficulties experienced by a quite separate group of children.

*Classical autism/classically autistic* are phrases used to describe autistic children whose particular pattern of difficulty corresponds closely to textbook description and who display many features of the syndrome in clear form (cf. *Kanner's syndrome* and *Nuclear autism*).

*Early infantile/childhood autism* are expansions of the label 'autism' and are its full title. Both were used originally by Kanner to draw attention to the age of onset of the difficulties.

*Kanner's syndrome* is a similar label to classical autism in that it refers to children for whom the diagnosis is very clear.

*Nuclear autism* is another way of describing children with many highly typical features of the syndrome. Epidemiological studies are at their most consistent when their findings are compared for cases of nuclear autism.

*Psychosis*: Within the classification systems used in child psychiatry, autism is viewed as one of the psychoses of childhood. The term 'childhood psychosis' does not therefore necessarily specify that a child suffers from autism.

*Psychotic*: Autistic children are sometimes described as showing 'psychotic behaviour' and what is generally meant here is that the behaviour is exceptionally extreme in its intensity or very inaccessible to adult understanding or intervention. 'Psychotic' does not specify a particular set of behaviours but says something about their quality.

## Further Reading

Wing, L. (ed.) (1976) *Early Childhood Autism* (2nd edn), Oxford: Pergamon Press
Rutter, M. and Shopler, E. (eds) *Autism: A Reappraisal of Concepts and Treatment*, New York: Plenum Press

In addition to the above books, which provide comprehensive source coverage, current research reports are published in the *Journal of Autism and Developmental Disorders*, Plenum Press 1970 onwards (four times annually).

The National Autistic Society
276 Willesden Lane
London NW2 5RB
Tel: 01 451 3844

also produces a range of pamphlets and papers on a variety of subjects, and acts as an information source for parents and professionals concerned with autistic children and adults.

# References

Ballantyne, J. (1977) *Deafness*, Edinburgh and London: Churchill Livingstone

Benedict, H. (1979) 'Early lexical development: comprehension and production', *Journal of Child Language, 6*, 183-200

British Association of Teachers of the Deaf (BATOD) (1981) 'Audiological definitions and forms for recording audiometric information', *Journal of the British Association of Teachers of the Deaf, 5*, 83-7

—— (1984) '1983 Survey on staffing, salaries, numbers of hearing impaired children, and use of manual communication', *Journal of the British Association of Teachers of the Deaf, 8*, 11-15

Butler, D. (1979) *Cushla and Her Books*, London: Hodder & Stoughton

—— (1980) *Babies Need Books*, New York: Atheneum

Butterfield, E.C. (1961) 'A provocative case of over-achievement by a mongoloid', *American Journal of Mental Deficiency, 66*, 444-8

Carr, J. (1970) 'Mental and motor development in young mongol children', *Journal of Mental Deficiency Research, 14*, 205

Conrad, R. (1979) *The Deaf Schoolchild: Language and Cognitive Function*, London: Harper & Row

Creak, M. (1961) 'Schizophrenic syndrome in children', *British Medical Journal, 2*, 889-90

Crystal, D. (1976) *Child Language, Learning and Linguistics*, London: Edward Arnold

—— (1980) *Introduction to Language Pathology*, London: Edward Arnold

Cullinan, T.R. (1977) 'The epidemiology of visual disability: studies of visually disabled people in the community', *Health Services Research Unit Report No. 28*, Centre for Research in Social Sciences, University of Kent

Davie, R., Butler, N. and Goldstein, H. (1972) *From Birth to Seven*, London: Longman

Department of Education and Science (1972) *The Education of the Visually Handicapped (The Vernon Report)*, London: HMSO

—— (1978) *Special Educational Needs. Report of the Committee of Enquiry into the Education of Handicapped Children and Young People (The Warnock Report)*, London: HMSO

Fraiberg, S. (1968) *The Magic Years: Understanding and Handling the Problems of Early Childhood*, London: Methuen

Gillham, B. (1979) *The First Words Language Programme*, London: Allen & Unwin and Beaconsfield Press

—— (1983) *Two Words Together*, London: Allen & Unwin

Gould, J. (1976) 'Language development and non-verbal skills in severely mentally retarded children: An epidemiological study', *Journal of Mental Deficiency Research, 20*, 129-46

Gregory, S. (1976) *The Deaf Child and His Family*, London: Allen & Unwin

Hutchinson, D. (1982) *Work Preparation for the Handicapped*, Croom Helm Special Education Series, London: Croom Helm

Jamieson, M., Partlett, M. and Pocklington, K. (1977) *Towards Integration: A study of blind and partially sighted children in ordinary schools* Windsor: NFER-Nelson

Jones, P. and Cregan, A. (1986) *Sign and Symbol Communication for Mentally Handicapped People* London: Croom Helm

Kanner, L. (1943) 'Autistic disturbances of affective contact', *Nervous Child, 2*, 217-50

Luria, A.R. (1961) *The Role of Speech in the Regulation of Normal and Abnormal Behaviour* Oxford: Pergamon Press

Masidlover, M. (1979) 'The Derbyshire Language Scheme: Remedial teaching for language delayed children', *Child: Care, Health and Development, 5*, 9-16

Millard, D.M. (1984) *Daily Living with a Handicapped Child*, Croom Helm Special Education Series, London: Croom Helm

Mittler, P. and Berry, P. (1977) Chapter in P. Mittler (ed) *Research to Practice in Mental Retardation Vol II Education and Training*, Baltimore: University Park Press

Newson, E. (1977) 'Diagnosis and early problems of autistic children', *Communication, II*, 3, 43-8

Rendle-Short, J. (1971) 'A paediatrician's approach to autism' in M. Ruttler (ed.) *Infantile Autism, Concepts, Characteristics and Treatment*, Edinburgh and London: Churchill Livingstone

Stevenson, J. and Richman, N. (1976) 'The prevalence of language delay in a population of three-year-old children and its association with general retardation', *Developmental Medicine and Child Neurology, 18*, 433-41

Swann, W. and Mittler, P. (1976) 'Language abilities of ESN(S) pupils', *Special Education: Forward Trends, 3*, 24-7

Tooze, D. (1981) *Independence Training for Visually Handicapped Children*, Croom Helm Special Education Series, London: Croom Helm

Vygotsky, L.S. (1962) *Thought and Language*, Cambridge, Mass: MIT Press

World Health Organization (1980) *International Classification of Impairments, Disabilities and Handicaps*, Geneva: WHO

# Notes on Contributors

*Bill Gillham* is Course Director of the MSc in Educational Psychology at Strathclyde University.

*Juliet Bishop* and *Susan Gregory* are Research Officers in the MRC Deafness Research Unit at Nottingham University.

*Allan Dodds* is Research Officer in the Blind Mobility Research Unit at Nottingham University.

*Ruth Gillham* is Senior Clinical Psychologist, specialising in neuropsychology, at the Southern General Hospital, Glasgow.

*Derek Wilson* is Educational Psychologist in the Nottinghamshire Schools Psychological Service, and former Head of Sutherland House School for Autistic Children.

# Index